MODERN TIMES

The United States since 1945

D. B. O'Callaghan

LONGMAN

LONGMAN GROUP LIMITED
Longman House
Burnt Mill, Harlow, Essex, CM20 2JE, England
and Associated Companies throughout the World.

First published 1983
Second impression 1986
ISBN 0 582 22181 1

Set in 11/12 pt. Baskerville, Linotron 202

Produced by Longman Group (FE) Ltd
Printed in Hong Kong

For Irene with love

Contents

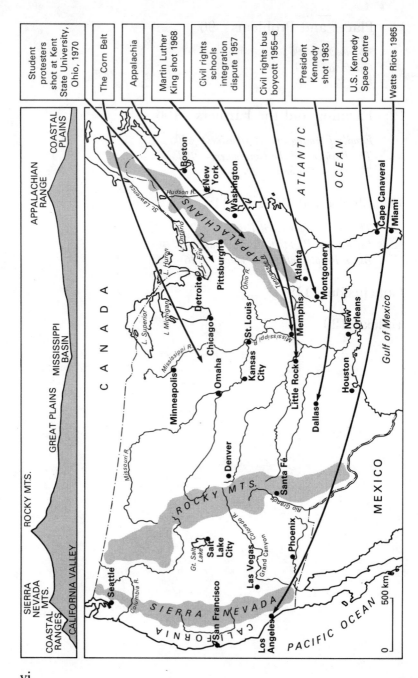

Student protesters shot at Kent State University, Ohio, 1970

The Corn Belt

Appalachia

Martin Luther King shot 1968

Civil rights schools integration dispute 1957

Civil rights bus boycott 1955–6

President Kennedy shot 1963

U.S. Kennedy Space Centre

Watts Riots 1965

SIERRA NEVADA

COASTAL RANGES

CALIFORNIA VALLEY

ROCKY MTS.

GREAT PLAINS

MISSISSIPPI BASIN

APPALACHIAN RANGE

COASTAL PLAINS

CANADA

ATLANTIC OCEAN

Boston
New York
Washington
Hudson R.
St. Lawrence
L. Ontario
L. Erie
L. Huron
L. Michigan
L. Superior
Detroit
Pittsburgh
APPALACHIANS
Chicago
St. Louis
Ohio R.
Minneapolis
Mississippi R.
Omaha
Kansas City
Missouri R.
Atlanta
Memphis
Tennessee R.
Montgomery
Little Rock
New Orleans
Houston
Dallas
Cape Canaveral
Miami
Gulf of Mexico
Denver
Santa Fé
ROCKY MTS.
Rio Grande
Salt Lake City
Gt. Salt Lake
Las Vegas
Colorado R.
Grand Canyon
Phoenix
MEXICO
Seattle
Columbia R.
San Francisco
Los Angeles
SIERRA NEVADA
CALIFORNIA
PACIFIC OCEAN

0   500 km

1 Ends and Beginnings

Truman Takes Over

'Boys, if you ever pray, pray for me now. I feel as if the sun, the stars and the moon have all fallen on top of me.' The man who said this was a stocky bespectacled former shopkeeper from a small town on the farmlands of America's midwest. His name was Harry S. Truman and he was speaking to a group of reporters on an April day in 1945. The day before he had suddenly become the most powerful man in the world — the President of the United States of America.

Six months earlier, in November 1944, the American people had gone to the polling booths to elect a president. For the fourth time running they had chosen Franklin Roosevelt, the man who had led the United States in peace and war since the early 1930s. Harry Truman was Roosevelt's Vice-President. This position was not as important as it sounds for vice-presidents of the United States have very little power. One holder of the post summed up its importance in these blunt words — 'It isn't worth a pitcher of warm spit.'

But by 1945 Roosevelt was a sick man. On the morning of 12 April he had a severe stroke and within hours he was dead. When an American president dies in office like this his place is taken by the Vice-President. That was how Harry Truman became President of the United States.

Most Americans knew very little about their new President. What kind of person was he? What was his background? In the summer of 1945 American newspapers and magazines did their best to answer these questions. They told their readers that the President was sixty years old; that

Opposite: The United States of America

1

he was the son of a farmer; that he was devoted to his wife and their only daughter; that he liked music; that he was in the habit of getting up early and taking a brisk walk before starting work. Facts such as these gradually built up a picture of the new President. It showed an ordinary kind of man with homely habits and, perhaps, rather limited abilities.

But the picture was not complete. For Harry Truman was to show that although he might be ordinary in some ways, in others he was quite extraordinary. In particular, he could make quick, firm decisions. In later years one of his chief advisers and supporters, Dean Acheson, said that what he most admired about Truman was his: 'capacity to understand complex questions and to decide. This is one of the rarest qualities possessed by man...Mr. Truman...listened intently to the arguments; and then he decided, clearly and firmly.' In the years ahead Truman's ability to decide 'clearly and firmly' was to be tested many times.

Uniting the Nations?

President Truman's first task was to lead the United States through the final stages of the Second World War. In Europe Adolf Hitler's Germany was crumbling into defeat and the fighting was almost over. Early in April 1945, in an underground hideout deep beneath the ruins of Berlin, Hitler shot himself and his armies laid down their arms. On 8 May 1945, less than a month after Harry Truman had become President of the United States, bonfires blazed and people danced in the streets to celebrate the end of the war in Europe.

From April until June, while all this was happening in Europe, there was an important conference going on in the American city of San Francisco. Its purpose was to set up a new international organization called the United Nations. The main aim of the United Nations (U.N.) was to keep the world at peace in the years ahead. Delegates from fifty nations met to discuss how this could best be done.

It was finally decided that the new organization should have three main parts. First the Secretariat was set up. The job of the Secretariat was to organize the meetings and

The founding of the United Nations Organization, 1945. As fighting ends in a war-ruined Europe, hopes for a more peaceful future dawn in San Francisco

everyday business of the U.N. It was headed by an official called the Secretary General. Then there was the General Assembly. This was a sort of parliament where international problems of all kinds could be discussed. Every member nation of the U.N. sent one representative to the Assembly. The great powers, like the United States and the Soviet Union, thought they should have more say than small countries in any decisions taken by the U.N. So the General Assembly was not given any real powers to take action. This was left to the third main part of the organization, the Security Council.

The Security Council of the U.N. had five permanent members — the United States, the Soviet Union, Britain, France and China — and six others who served on it for two years at a time. The Council was intended to be responsible for keeping the world at peace. For example, it could order

3

action to be taken against any nation that seemed to be threatening war. But for this to happen all five permanent members of the Security Council had to agree. This meant that any of these permanent members could stop the U.N. from acting whenever it wished. This power of veto, as it was called, was one upon which both the United States and the Soviet Union insisted. It meant that the success of the United Nations depended more than anything else upon co-operation between these two countries, by far the strongest in the world. But soon they became increasingly suspicious of each other. In the United Nations nearly everything that one of them suggested was opposed by the other. This made it almost impossible for the Security Council to do its job.

Conference in Potsdam

The Soviet Union had suffered terribly at the hands of the Germans in the Second World War. Twenty million of her people had died. Her richest farm lands and most modern cities had been destroyed. The Russian leader, Joseph Stalin, was determined that this should never happen again. Long before the fighting ended he told his American and British allies that after the war he wanted a protective screen of friendly nations between the Soviet Union and Germany. The United States and Britain agreed to this. In the spring of 1945, however, it seemed increasingly clear that by 'friendly' nations, Stalin meant nations with Communist-controlled governments who would do what he told them. In Poland, the country occupying the key position between the Soviet Union and Germany, he arrested many of the chief non-communist leaders even before the German surrender.

When President Truman heard of this he was both angry and alarmed. The Russians had agreed earlier that they would allow the people of the lands that they freed from German rule to choose new governments for themselves, without interference. Truman sent for Molotov, the Russian Foreign Minister, and told him off. 'I have never been spoken to like that in my life', complained the Russian. 'Carry out your agreements and you won't get spoken to like that again', snapped Truman.

'The Big Three' — Churchill, Truman, Stalin — pose for photographers at the Potsdam Conference, 1945. Away from the cameras things were less friendly

In July Truman came face to face with Stalin himself. The leaders of the principal countries responsible for defeating Hitler — the Allied powers as they were called — held a conference in the German town of Potsdam, not far from Berlin. The British Prime Minister, Winston Churchill, was also at the first meetings, though he was later replaced by Clement Attlee, who became Prime Minister when the Labour Party won the British General Election of 1945.

The Allied leaders reached a number of agreements at Potsdam. They agreed about disarming Germany, about making the Germans pay for the damage they had done (reparations), about frontiers and about how the Germans should be governed for the time being. But the atmosphere was far from friendly.

The trouble was that Truman and Stalin did not trust one another. Each thought that the other was out to deceive and trick him. Stalin was a Communist. He believed that a nation's land, factories, mines — all its 'means of production' as they are called — should be owned and run by the state, as they were in the Soviet Union. The United States of America, by contrast, was a capitalist country. The whole American way of life was based upon the means of producing wealth being owned by private individuals and firms. In government too there were big differences. In the United States

5

people had some choice in deciding who should rule the country. In the Soviet Union there was no choice, for the Communist Party was the only party allowed and anyone who opposed it was likely to be arrested and thrown into prison.

To Truman, the Communist way of running a country seemed to rob people of their freedom as individuals. He thought communism was evil and was determined to stop it from spreading. For his part, Stalin disliked American capitalism just as much as Truman disliked Russian communism. He feared it too, for he believed that America's capitalist leaders would like to crush communism to stop it spreading from the Soviet Union to other parts of the world. Now that Germany had been beaten Stalin was afraid that the Americans might turn on the Soviet Union and attack her.

When Truman returned to the United States from Potsdam he was convinced that Stalin was planning to spread communism to as many countries as possible. Whether the Russians had such a plan is something that is still argued about now. Some people think that Truman was right and that Stalin was plotting to create a world dominated by communism. Others believe that he was wrong and that all Stalin wanted was to make the Soviet Union safe from attack. One thing was certain however — Truman and Stalin went home from Potsdam full of suspicion and distrust of one another.

Hiroshima

On 16 July 1945, the day after his arrival in Potsdam for the conference with Stalin and Churchill, President Truman received an important message from the United States. It told him that the world's first atomic bomb had been successfully tested earlier that same day in the deserts of New Mexico. After years of research Allied scientists had released what Truman described later as 'the basic powers of the universe'. They had created a weapon of unimaginable power, one that made all others seem about as dangerous as catapults:

The key to end the still continuing war against Japan, Germany's ally, was now in Truman's hands. On 24 July he told Stalin about the atomic bomb and two days later the Japanese government was given a warning — to surrender immediately or to face 'prompt and utter destruction'. When the Japanese leaders failed to give a clear reply Truman ordered an atomic bomb to be dropped on the city of Hiroshima.

At fifteen minutes past seven on the morning of 6 August 1945 a solitary American B.29 bomber flew high over Hiroshima and dropped the bomb. Forty-five seconds later it exploded. A great ball of purple fire turned the centre of Hiroshima into a raging furnace and a mushroom-shaped cloud of boiling smoke and debris climbed thousands of metres into the sky above the city. Thousands of people died instantly, their bodies turned to vapour by the incredible heat. Thousands more were to die later from their injuries and some were still suffering more than thirty years later. Three days after the first bomb another was dropped on the Japanese city of Nagasaki, with equally devastating effects.

The people of the Allied countries had mixed feelings about dropping the atomic bombs. On the one hand they were delighted that the war with Japan would now end quickly, without the loss of more Allied soldiers' lives. On the other hand they feared for the future. A British magazine wrote:

'Thousands of people died instantly, thousands more were to die later from their injuries'. Survivors of the atomic bombing of Nagasaki, 1945

'Henceforward all men everywhere will be living on the edge of a volcano.'

Ever since the destruction of Hiroshima and Nagasaki there have been arguments about whether Truman was right to use such a terrible weapon. He himself had no doubts on the issue. 'I regarded the bomb as a military weapon and never had any doubt that it should be used', he wrote later.

The use of the bomb certainly achieved its declared objective of ending the war quickly. Within days of the bombings of Hiroshima and Nagasaki the Japanese government surrendered. But since then some experts have argued that in August 1945 the Japanese were about to surrender anyway. The bomb was used, they say, not just to defeat the Japanese but to frighten the Russians. Truman's idea was to show Stalin what a terrible weapon the Americans, and only the Americans, now had. Then the Russians would be more likely to make a genuine attempt to keep the peace in the years to come.

There may be some truth in this belief. Even if there is, Truman's supporters claim that his decision to drop the bomb may still, in the long run, have saved more lives than it destroyed. For the United States and the Soviet Union dangerous years of tension and conflict lay ahead. How long, ask the President's supporters, would they have held themselves back from fighting one another without the terrible sufferings of the people of Hiroshima and Nagasaki to remind them of the costs of nuclear war?

The Iron Curtain

In the months which followed the Potsdam Conference of July 1945 relations between the United States and the Soviet Union had got steadily worse. The main area they disagreed about was Eastern Europe, particularly those countries like Poland and Hungary which Russian soldiers had occupied after driving out the Germans. Stalin had made it clear at Potsdam that he was prepared to allow free elections in these countries only if the voters did not elect anti-Russian governments.

During 1945 Stalin's victorious armies had seen to it that

this condition was fulfilled. In almost every country occupied by the Soviet Union pro-Russian rulers took over. Some of them were Communists, some of them were non-Communists. But Stalin soon decided that the only safely pro-Russian government was a Communist government. He started getting rid of any East European leaders who would not obey him.

On 5 March 1946 Winston Churchill spoke at a meeting in Fulton, a town in President Truman's home state of Missouri. With Truman nodding agreement on the platform beside him, he gave out a sombre warning:

'Nobody knows what Soviet Russia intends to do in the future, or what are the limits, if any, to their expansive tendencies. From . . . the Baltic to . . . the Adriatic, an Iron Curtain has descended. . . . Behind that line all the capitals of the ancient states of central and eastern Europe . . . are subject to a high and increasing measure of control from Moscow. The Communist parties, which were very small in those eastern states of Europe, have been raised to power far beyond their numbers and are seeking everywhere to obtain totalitarian control. . . . Whatever conclusions may be drawn from these facts — and facts they are — this is certainly not the liberated Europe we fought to build up.'

The Truman Doctrine

By 1947 Churchill's 'Iron Curtain' had become more than a figure of speech; it was a physical reality (see map on page 17). Across hundreds of kilometres of fields and forests, minefields and barbed-wire fences sealed off the Communist-ruled peoples in the East of Europe from the non-Communist nations of the West.

In the south-east corner of Europe lay the poor and mountainous country of Greece. Here fierce fighting was raging, between a royalist government friendly towards Britain and the United States, and an army of Communist rebels. British soldiers were helping the royalists. In 1947, however, Britain told the American government she could no longer afford to do this and would soon have to withdraw her troops and leave the royalists to face the Communists alone.

Truman knew that the withdrawal of British troops might well mean an eventual Communist victory in Greece. This would bring Communist power to the shores of the Mediterranean Sea, an area which had so far been free from it. Dean Acheson, one of Truman's chief advisers, had been arguing for some time that the Americans should adopt a policy of 'containing' communism — that is, of taking action to stop it from spreading further. At the first opportunity, argued Acheson, the United States should make some kind of dramatic gesture to show that she would no longer stand by while Communists took over in still more countries. He advised the President that the crisis in Greece was just the opportunity that the American government needed; and the President agreed.

On 12 March 1947 Truman announced the new policy of containment in a speech to the American Congress. He said that the United States would give money, food and equipment to help the government of Greece to prevent a Communist take-over. He also made it clear that the United States would give similar aid to any other country in such a position.

Critics of Truman have said since that this policy — the 'Truman Doctrine' as it was quickly called — amounted to a sort of declaration of war on the Soviet Union. It was a new kind of war, a 'Cold War', in which, although there was no fighting, there was bound to be constant suspicion and quarrelling between the United States and the Soviet Union. Supporters of Truman's action reject this charge. They say that the main cause of the outbreak of the Cold War was the expansionist way the Russians had acted in Eastern Europe. They claim that the Truman Doctrine, by contrast, was essentially a defensive movement, aimed at keeping things as they were rather than at spreading American power.

But whoever was mainly responsible for starting the Cold War, one thing was certain: 1947 saw the world firmly divided into two mutually hostile armed camps. This division was to dominate world affairs for more than the next quarter of a century.

2 Cold War in Europe

Continent in Ruins

'I never saw such destruction. A more depressing sight than that of the ruined buildings was the long, never-ending procession of old men, women and children . . . carrying, pushing or pulling what was left of their belongings. I was thankful that the United States had been spared the unbelievable devastation of this war.'

These words were written by President Truman in the summer of 1945 after his visit to Europe. He was writing about Germany but he could have been describing almost any European country at that time. It was as if a great tidal wave had swept across the Continent destroying everything in its path. Sufficient clothing to keep warm, enough food to stay

Germany 1946. The war ended a year ago, but people still queue among the ruins for handouts of soup

alive, a home to live in, a place to work — in 1945 millions of Europe's people lacked some or all of these things.

Two years later things were little better. Many people were becoming desperate. In France and Italy the local Communist parties won lots of support by promising sweeping reforms to make things better. This worried Truman and in the summer of 1947 his government put forward a plan which he hoped would both help the people of Europe and stop the spread of communism at the same time.

The Marshall Plan

The United States was the only country in the world whose people were better off after the Second World War than they had been before. In 1947 she had plenty of all the things that Europe lacked — food, fuel, machinery, raw materials. The trouble was that Europe was too poor to buy them.

To get round this problem the Secretary of State, General George Marshall, the man in charge of the United States' dealings with other countries, offered to provide the countries of Europe with the things they needed as a gift. The offer of help was open to all the countries of Europe, including the Communist ones. 'Our policy is directed not against any country or doctrine, but against hunger, poverty, desperation, chaos', he claimed.

But the Russians refused to have anything to do with Marshall's Plan. They said that the Plan's main purpose was to make profits for American manufacturers, and they did not allow any of the other countries on their side of the Iron Curtain to take part in it either.

The hostile attitude of the Russians was no surprise to Marshall. He was convinced that Stalin was deliberately waiting for the economic life of Western Europe to collapse so that the voters would sweep Communists into power.

It was partly to prevent this that he and Dean Acheson suggested the idea of the Marshall Plan to President Truman in the first place. Its underlying political aim was the same as that of the Truman Doctrine — to stop the spread of communism. As Truman himself put it later, the Marshall Plan

'It was like giving a desperately sick person a blood transfusion'. Marshall Aid arrives in Britain, 1949

and the Truman Doctrine were 'two halves of the same walnut'.

This does not necessarily mean that the sympathy that Truman and Marshall expressed for the sufferings of the people of Europe was not genuine. Years later Truman spoke of the Plan to a television interviewer in these words:

'In the winter and spring of 1947 . . . I doubt if things in Europe have ever been worse, in the Middle Ages maybe but not in modern times. People were starving and they were cold because there wasn't enough coal, and tuberculosis was breaking out. There had been food riots in France and Italy, everywhere. And as if that wasn't bad enough, that winter turned out to be the coldest in history, almost. Something had to be done. The British were broke; they couldn't help the people on the Continent. The United States had to do it, had to do it all and the Congress had to be persuaded that it was necessary. . . . We went ahead and did what had to be done, and the Marshall Plan saved Europe, and that's something I am glad I had some part in helping accomplish.'

13

Truman was right. The Marshall Plan did save Europe. From 1948 onwards millions of dollars worth of American food, raw materials and machinery flowed across the Atlantic Ocean. It was like giving a desperately sick person a blood transfusion. By 1950 the nations of Western Europe were at last well on the way to recovery.

The Marshall Plan also benefited the United States. It gave her farmers buyers for their produce. It kept her factories busy, turning out the manufactured goods that Europe needed. It achieved its political aim too. The spread of communism was halted, for as life got better in the West, support for local Communist parties fell sharply.

But although the United States gained a lot from the Marshall Plan, the people of Europe gained still more. It gave them food and fuel, homes and work. Most important of all it gave them hope and confidence for the future.

Airlift to Berlin

When the fighting in Europe ended in the spring of 1945 soldiers from each of the Allied powers — the United States, Soviet Union, Britain and France — took over and occupied one of the four zones into which Germany was then divided. The idea was that this would only be temporary. Once the Allies could agree on the details, they intended the whole country to be ruled again by one government. Each of them wanted to be sure, however, that any united Germany that might be created would be friendly towards them.

Stalin felt especially strongly about this. The Soviet Union had suffered more than anyone from the Germans. The only friendly Germany Stalin could think of was a Germany controlled by Communists, something which the United States, Britain and France were determined to prevent. The result was that little progress was made in the many discussions that were held about Germany's future.

By 1946 it was already becoming clear that not one but two Germanies were beginning to take shape — a Communist one in the east of the country and a non-Communist one in the west. Deep inside the Russian-controlled zone lay Berlin. Since Berlin was Germany's old capital it too had been divided between the Allies, into areas called sectors. To link the Western-controlled sectors of Berlin with the outside world the Russians had agreed to let goods and people pass freely through their zone of Germany.

By 1948 Berlin had become the main point of friction in the disagreements about Germany's future. The trouble came to a head over money. The Western Allies were eager to press ahead with rebuilding the German economy, for without German industrial production and German customers for their goods other European nations were finding it very difficult to get their economies going again. Before this problem could be solved, something had to be done about German money. In 1948 this was almost worthless. An ordinary factory worker earned between 75 and 100 marks a week. It would have cost him 25 marks to buy *one* cigarette.

To solve this situation the Western Allies announced that in their zones, from Sunday 20 June, all the old marks would be called in and a fresh start made with new currency.

The Russians were furious. Stalin's Foreign Minister, Molotov, had already attacked the Western plans to rebuild Germany's industries. He complained:

'American Senators and businessmen are lording it in the western zones and helping the American monopolies to penetrate ever deeper into the industry and banks of western Germany. This plan reflects the desire to convert western Germany into a base for extending the influence of American imperialism in Europe.'

On 24 June 1948, a few days after the new money came into use, the Russians stopped all traffic between west Germany and west Berlin. To start with they may have intended simply to make things difficult for the Western Powers in order to persuade them to change their economic policies. But soon they became more ambitious. They blocked all the roads, railway lines and canals linking Berlin with the Western zones of Germany. Their aim was to make it impossible for the Western Allies to supply the 2 million people living in their sectors of Berlin with sufficient food and fuel. They hoped that this would force the Western troops and officials to pack up and go, leaving the city to the Russians.

15

Berlin 1948. Unloading 20 tonnes of flour, airlifted into Berlin by American transport

The leaders of the United States and Britain felt that they could not back down from this challenge. They decided to keep the city going by sending in everything it needed by air. Fleets of American and British planes began to fly supplies into Berlin. This 'airlift' went on for almost a year. On its busiest day nearly 14,000 aircraft landed on the city's airfields. Over 2 million tonnes of supplies were delivered, including a daily average of 5,000 tonnes of coal.

Stalin did not want to turn the Cold War into a hot one, so the Russians did not attack the American and British supply planes as they flew along the air corridors with their loads of food and coal. For the same reason the Western Allies decided not to send armed convoys to force a way into Berlin by road. By the end of 1948 the Russians knew they were beaten. In February 1949 secret talks began and in May Stalin called off the blockade.

The Berlin blockade finished all hope of uniting Germany under one government. In 1949 the Western Powers joined their zones together to form the Federal German Republic, or West Germany. Stalin replied by turning the Russian zone into the German Democratic Republic, or East Germany.

Opposite: Conflict and Cold War in Europe

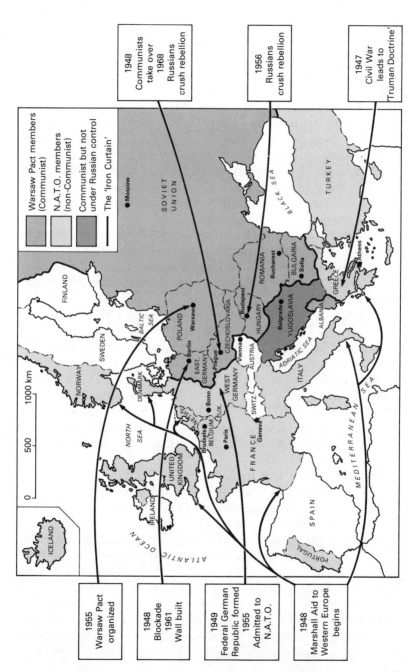

1948
Communists take over
1968
Russians crush rebellion

1956
Russians crush rebellion

1947
Civil War leads to
'Truman Doctrine'

Warsaw Pact members (Communist)

N.A.T.O. members (non-Communist)

Communist but not under Russian control

The 'Iron Curtain'

1955
Warsaw Pact organized

1948
Blockade
1961
Wall built

1949
Federal German Republic formed
1955
Admitted to N.A.T.O.

1948
Marshall Aid to Western Europe begins

ICELAND

ATLANTIC OCEAN

IRELAND

UNITED KINGDOM

NORTH SEA

NORWAY

SWEDEN

FINLAND

BALTIC SEA

DENMARK

NETHS.

Brussels
BELGIUM
LUX.

Paris

FRANCE

SWITZ.
Geneva

SPAIN

PORTUGAL

MEDITERRANEAN SEA

EAST GERMANY
Berlin

Bonn
WEST GERMANY

Prague
CZECHOSLOVAKIA

POLAND
Warsaw

Vienna
AUSTRIA

Budapest
HUNGARY

Belgrade
YUGOSLAVIA

ADRIATIC SEA

ITALY

ALBANIA

GREECE
Athens

ROMANIA
Bucharest

BULGARIA
Sofia

BLACK SEA

TURKEY

SOVIET UNION

Moscow

0   500   1000 km

17

The Birth of N.A.T.O.

In the years after 1945 the non-Communist governments of Western Europe looked uneasily at the huge Russian armies grouped just behind the barbed-wire and the minefields of the Iron Curtain. They feared that at any moment Stalin might order his soldiers forward to overrun them. In February 1948 their fears increased. With Russian support local Communists took over Czechoslovakia. In June Stalin started the blockade of Berlin. Western leaders became convinced that the Russians were getting ready to attack.

These events convinced President Truman that Western Europe needed more than economic aid to regain its strength and confidence. In 1949 he invited most of the nations there to join the United States in setting up the North Atlantic Treaty Organization (N.A.T.O.). This was an alliance of nations who agreed to stand by one another against threats from the Russians and set up combined armed forces to do this.

The North Atlantic Treaty was signed in Washington in April 1949. The following September its importance was underlined by a brief statement from President Truman. 'We have evidence', he announced, 'that within recent weeks an atomic explosion occurred in the U.S.S.R.' The evidence Truman was referring to was a radio-active air sample which an American patrol aircraft had collected high over the Pacific Ocean a few weeks earlier. The sample contained drifting fall-out material from 'Joe One', the Soviet Union's first atomic bomb.

The news that the Russians too could now make atomic bombs persuaded the American Congress to vote many millions of dollars to equip N.A.T.O.'s armed forces. In 1951 General Eisenhower, one of the United States' best-known generals of the Second World War, was placed in command of these forces. Soon there were many thousands of American fighting men in Europe once more. But although N.A.T.O. depended heavily on the United States for most of its men, money and equipment, all its members made some contribution. Even West Germany was soon providing a few soldiers.

In reply to N.A.T.O. the Russians organized the Warsaw Pact. This was an alliance of the Communist nations of

N.A.T.O. forces practise their skills. Refuelling at sea during a sea-air exercise in the 1950s

Eastern Europe who set up combined armed forces under Russian leadership in 1955.

By the middle of the 1950s Western Europe's economic recovery was well under way. The protection of N.A.T.O. gave Western countries more confidence in their ability to stand up to any attempts to spread communism by force. True, Europe was dangerously divided into two hostile and heavily armed camps. But a kind of balance of power had been achieved between the Americans and the Russians. Many people felt safer than they had done a few years earlier in the uneasy and insecure atmosphere of the late 1940s.

Winston Churchill had no doubts about who was responsible for this. At a meeting in 1952 he summed up many people's feelings when he told President Truman:

'The last time you and I sat across a conference table was at Potsdam. I must confess, Sir, I held you in very low regard. ...I misjudged you badly. Since that time you, more than any other man, have saved Western civilisation.'

3 Cold War in the East

Reconstruction in Japan

At the end of August 1945 American troops began landing in Japan. Their leader was General Douglas MacArthur, who had commanded the United States' forces in the Pacific war and who now became the unquestioned ruler of the people of Japan.

MacArthur was a remarkable person. He was able and brave, yet at the same time vain and theatrical. People either admired him greatly or disliked him greatly. But even MacArthur's enemies had little but praise for his achieve-

MacArthur and Hirohito, the new and the old rulers of Japan, Tokyo 1945

ments in Japan. He found the country in ruins; 'devastated, hopeless, flat broke and leaderless', as one observer described it. He left it only a few years later with a new democratic system of government, a modernized social life and an economy that was already on the way to giving its people the highest standard of living in Asia.

MacArthur set up his headquarters near Emperor Hirohito's palace in Tokyo. The Japanese people still worshipped Hirohito like a god and MacArthur realized that to govern Japan effectively he had to get the Emperor's co-operation. So he won the support of Hirohito and used it to persuade the Japanese people to accept sweeping changes in their old ways of life. All adults were given the vote and a national Parliament called the 'Diet' was elected. Workers were encouraged to form trade unions. Rich land-owners were made to give up vast areas of land which the government then sold at low prices, to provide millions of small farmers with their own farms. Reforms like these laid the foundations for great changes in Japanese life in the years after 1945.

Under MacArthur's control, the people of Japan worked hard to rebuild their shattered country. They were helped by money, food and equipment from the United States which poured into Japan, especially after 1948. There was a good reason for this. These years at the end of the 1940s saw a Communist government gain control of China, Japan's giant neighbour (see page 22). The Cold War seemed to be spreading to Asia. The Americans decided that they needed a strong and friendly ally in the area so they did everything they could to build up the strength of the new Japan as quickly as possible. Their need for a strong Japan became still more urgent in 1950, when American troops became involved in a war to prevent Communists taking over the nearby country of Korea (see page 24). Japan quickly became the main supply base for the American forces in Korea.

In 1951 the United States and Japan signed a treaty which officially ended the American occupation and government of Japan. However, under an agreement with the new Japanese government the Americans still kept troops there and independent Japan was closely allied to the United States.

The United States since 1945

Revolution in China

On 1 October 1949 an important ceremony took place in a huge square in the centre of the ancient Chinese city of Peking. In front of a wildly enthusiastic crowd the Chinese People's Republic was proclaimed. The world's largest nation now had a Communist government.

Communist ideas had spread to China from Russia. In the 1920s the Chinese ruler, a dictator named Chiang Kai-shek, had struggled without success to crush the Chinese Communists. Then in the 1930s China was attacked by Japan. Chiang and the Communist leader, Mao Tse-tung, reluctantly made a truce. They agreed to stop fighting one another until the Japanese were defeated.

China's struggle against Japan became part of the Second World War from 1941 onwards. When Japan surrendered in 1945 Chiang ruled most of China's cities. But vast areas of the countryside were controlled by Mao. The Americans tried to help Chiang to gain full control. The country was soon in the middle of a bloody civil war. Chiang had big armies, well armed with all the latest American equipment, and most people expected him to win the war easily. But millions of ordinary Chinese were tired of being badly treated by Chiang's government. As Mao's armies marched across China the country folk welcomed them. Even Chiang's soldiers deserted him. Whole armies went over to Mao, taking their weapons and equipment with them.

By 1949 the struggle was over and Mao and his Communist armies were the masters of China. Chiang fled across the sea to the island of Formosa, or Taiwan as it is now called. Only American warships prevented Mao's armies from following and crushing him.

The help that the Americans had given to Chiang left the victorious Mao with strong feelings of resentment and suspicion towards the United States. Within a year these feelings were to help to bring open warfare between American and Chinese soldiers in the neighbouring land of Korea.

Opposite: Conflict and Cold War in Asia

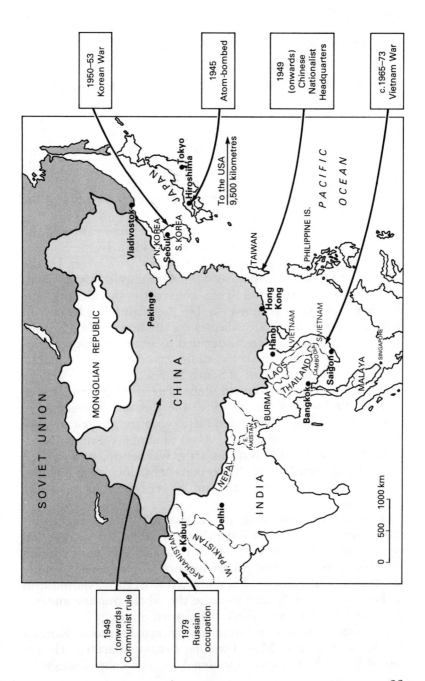

1950–53
Korean War

1945
Atom-bombed

1949
(onwards)
Chinese
Nationalist
Headquarters

c.1965–73
Vietnam War

SOVIET UNION

MONGOLIAN REPUBLIC

CHINA

Vladivostok

N.KOREA
Seoul
S.KOREA

JAPAN

Tokyo
Hiroshima

To the USA
9,500 kilometres

TAIWAN

PHILIPPINE IS.

PACIFIC

OCEAN

Peking

Hong
Kong

Hanoi
VIETNAM
N.VIETNAM
LAOS
S.VIETNAM
Saigon
CAMBODIA
THAILAND
Bangkok
BURMA
MALAYA
SINGAPORE

NEPAL
E.
PAKISTAN

INDIA

Delhi

Kabul
AFGHANISTAN
W. PAKISTAN

0   500   1000 km

1949
(onwards)
Communist rule

1979
Russian
occupation

23

War in Korea

Korea is a thumb-shaped peninsula which sticks out from the mainland of Asia towards Japan (see map on page 23). In 1945 American and Russian troops moved into the country and ended thirty years of Japanese colonial rule there. The two armies met in the middle of the country, at the 38th parallel of latitude. It was agreed that, for the moment, the Russians should run Korea north of the 38th parallel while the Americans ran the south. The next step would be for the people of Korea to elect a government of their own to run the whole country.

But the elections never took place. The Americans and the Russians withdrew but Korea stayed divided. In the South a government favoured by the Americans took over. In the North the Russians helped set up a Communist government. These two governments were constantly threatening one another, for each claimed to be the rightful ruler of all Korea. There were many clashes on the border. In 1950 the Communist North Koreans decided to settle the matter once and for all. On 25 June their soldiers crossed the 38th parallel in a full-scale invasion of South Korea.

President Truman immediately ordered American forces to help the South Koreans. With the Russian representative absent because of an earlier quarrel with the Americans, the Security Council of the U.N. voted to support Truman's action. A special United Nations army was set up, commanded by General MacArthur. Sixteen nations, including Britain, supplied troops for this army, but 90 per cent of its men were Americans.

At first the Communist armies swept all before them. But after three months of hard fighting the Americans had pushed them back across the 38th parallel and were driving into North Korea. The American aim was no longer simply to protect South Korea. They wanted to destroy communism in Korea completely and to unite the whole country under a government friendly towards the United States.

As American troops swept northwards towards Korea's border with China, Mao Tse-tung became alarmed. He believed that a Korea united under American control might be

Korea 1950. Refugees wait patiently by the roadside as an American convoy heads for the front line

used as a base for an attack on China. His Foreign Minister warned the Americans that the Chinese would not stand for this.

Truman was concerned at Mao's warning, but General MacArthur assured him that the Chinese were bluffing. MacArthur was wrong. When the warning was ignored Mao ordered thousands of experienced Chinese soldiers into action in Korea. Overnight the victorious American advance became a disorganized retreat. A new and more terrible war began. It was really a war between the United States and China, although neither country officially admitted this.

MacArthur soon came to believe that the only way for the Americans to win the war in Korea was to attack China itself. He suggested this to Truman, but the President turned down the idea for fear of starting another world war. MacArthur then tried to go over Truman's head. He issued statements to the newspapers criticizing the President's policy. Truman ordered him to be silent. When MacArthur refused he sacked him.

Years later Truman told an interviewer: 'I fired him because he wouldn't respect the authority of the President.' As Truman saw it, what was at stake was one of the basic principles of democratic government — that the first duty of a military leader is to obey the leaders elected by the people.

The sacking of MacArthur brought down a storm of abuse on Truman's head. Americans were tired of their sons being killed in Korea. At least, they argued, MacArthur's idea gave a hope of victory. All Truman seemed to be offering was a further never-ending waste of American lives and money. With bitter sarcasm they started to call the conflict 'Truman's War'.

When the sacked MacArthur returned to the United States he was greeted in city after city by hysterically cheering crowds. The climax came when, by special invitation, he defended his ideas in a dramatic speech to Congress.

But Truman too had his defenders, and as people calmed down they came to realize that he was probably right after all. Another famous general, Omar Bradley, reminded the American people that the Korean War was just part of the world-wide struggle then going on against communism. He pointed out that the Soviet Union, the strongest Communist nation, was not involved in it at all. A MacArthur-style showdown with the Chinese would, said Bradley, leave the Russians waiting on the sidelines while the United States became involved 'in the wrong war, at the wrong place, at the wrong time and with the wrong enemy'.

The Korean War dragged on bloodily for another two years. It ended at last in July 1953 after the newly elected President Eisenhower hinted that the Americans might use atomic weapons if the Chinese did not agree to a ceasefire. Korea remained divided along the 38th parallel, with its poor and bewildered people far worse off than when the fighting had started.

Thirty-three thousand Americans had died in Korea. Over 100,000 more had been wounded. Yet the Americans believed they had won a kind of victory. Communists everywhere, they claimed, had been shown that it did not pay to try to spread their rule by force. Containment had proved more expensive than anyone had expected — but it had worked.

McCarthyism

In summer 1949 the Russians exploded their first atomic bomb. At about the same time the armies of Mao Tse-tung finally won control of China. These two major successes for communism shifted the world's balance of power and made it clear that the United States was no longer all-powerful.

Many Americans were shocked and worried by this. They began to wonder if clever conspirators were at work, secretly undermining American strength and safety.

Such fears set the scene for the rise to public notice of a previously little-known senator named Joseph R. McCarthy, from the mid-western state of Wisconsin. On 9 February 1950 McCarthy made a speech in which he declared that the Federal Government was 'infested' with Communists. He held up a sheet of paper. 'I have here in my hand a list of 205 names known to the Secretary of State as members of the Communist Party who nevertheless are still working and shaping policy.'

McCarthy's accusation was a lie. A Senate committee set up to investigate his claim described it as 'a fraud and a hoax'. But people refused to listen. By this time fear of Communist plotting was spreading and McCarthy quickly became the most talked about man in the country. When the Korean War began later that same year still more people came to believe his claims that the United States was being betrayed.

McCarthy was quick to realize that he had found a way to get fame and power for himself. He started to lash out in every direction. He accused scientists, writers, university professors, diplomats, actors. American fears of communism grew so strong that many had their careers ruined. When McCarthy's victims denied his charges he simply moved on to fresh targets, his accusations growing steadily more sensational. The climax came when he accused perhaps the most respected of all living American leaders, General George Marshall, of being the organizer of a plot against the country.

Despite McCarthy's failure to produce proof, people thought that there must be some truth in the things he was saying because his lies were so big and his victims so well known. Other politicians recognized that his popularity could win them votes and, while they might despise him

America's 'witch hunter'. Senator Joseph McCarthy gives reporters another story

secretly, in public they often spoke out in his support. Years later President Truman said that to him this was the most disturbing thing about McCarthy's success. He went on: 'A man like that — it's like a sickness. It isn't going to disappear if you just ignore it. And ... the people who know a man like that is up to no good but who encourage him ... who'll do anything in the world to win an election. They're just as bad.'

The end of McCarthy's influence came in the summer of 1954. He started an investigation of the army. The proceedings were televised and for several weeks McCarthy's dark scowl and bullying manner, his disregard for both the truth and the rights of other people, were exposed for millions to see. When the investigation ended his spell was broken. People had at last seen him for what he was and although he went on issuing statements and making wild charges, the country no longer listened.

In 1957 McCarthy died. But he had done serious and lasting damage to America's reputation for justice and fair play. Some people wondered if the vein of intolerance that he had uncovered in the American people might emerge again the next time they became afraid.

4 A Balance of Terror

The H-bomb

From 1950 onwards scientists on both sides·of the 'Iron Curtain' were working hard to develop a weapon many times more powerful and destructive than the bombs that had devastated Hiroshima and Nagasaki. This new weapon was the hydrogen-bomb, or 'H-bomb' as it was called. The Americans tested their first H-bomb in 1952. The Russians followed suit in 1953. Although Britain produced a similar bomb in 1957, only the United States and the Soviet Union could afford the immense costs of continuing to produce the new weapons. The two 'superpowers' were now more powerful than ever.

One H-bomb contained five times the destructive power of the total of all the bombs dropped in five years of the Second World War. To many people this terrible destructive power seemed to threaten the whole existence of mankind. But to others the very destructiveness of the new bombs seemed to make them a force for peace. War, they hoped, would now become impossible for the simple reason that no one would dare to start one.

Not everyone agreed with this optimistic view. But one thing was sure. The fact that the United States and the Soviet Union both had hydrogen-bombs was to play a vital part in deciding how they behaved towards one another for years to come.

Eisenhower and Dulles

In November 1952 a test explosion of an American hydrogen bomb blasted an entire island out of the Pacific Ocean. In the same month the American people elected their new

Washington 1954. President Eisenhower (left) listens attentively to the views of his Secretary of State, John Foster Dulles

President. The man they chose to replace Truman was the Republican Dwight D. Eisenhower — popularly known as 'Ike'.

Eisenhower had been one of the most successful American generals of the Second World War and later had become the first commander of the armed forces of N.A.T.O. These posts had given him plenty of experience in dealing with the leaders of other countries. Despite this, for most of his presidency Eisenhower left the conduct of American foreign policy to John Foster Dulles, his Secretary of State.

Dulles was a man of strong moral convictions, who genuinely believed that communism was evil. Truman, he claimed, had not been tough enough with the Russians. His own idea was for the United States to take the offensive in the world-wide struggle against communism. Instead of being content simply to contain communism ('a cringing policy of the fearful', as he called it) the Americans should set out to 'liberate' nations already under Communist rule. 'You can count on us', he told the peoples of Eastern Europe in a broadcast in 1953.

In 1956 the people of Hungary put Dulles's promise to the

test. They rose in rebellion against their Communist rulers. When Russian tanks rolled in to crush them they sent out desperate appeals for help. The help never came. Thousands of refugees fled across the Iron Curtain to safety in the neighbouring country of Austria. 'We can never believe the west again', one of them sadly told a reporter.

Dulles failed to help the Hungarians because he knew that doing so would mean war with the Soviet Union. The devastation of nuclear war was, he decided, too high a price to pay for 'rolling back' the Iron Curtain. Instead, he intensified the Cold War. The policy of containment was extended to new areas of the world. In 1954, after the end of the war in Korea, Dulles set up the South East Asia Treaty Organization (S.E.A.T.O.). This was an alliance of anti-Communist nations, including three Asian ones, which Dulles hoped would halt the spread of communism in Asia just as N.A.T.O. had done in Europe. In 1955 he set up a similar alliance called the Central Treaty Organization (C.E.N.T.O.), designed to stop the spread of communism amongst the nations of the Middle East.

Brinkmanship and Massive Retaliation

'The ability to get to the verge without getting into war is the necessary art. If you cannot master it, you inevitably get into war. If you . . . are scared to go to the brink, you are lost.'

The speaker was John Foster Dulles in an interview printed in January 1956. By 'going to the brink' he meant that the American government should make it clear that it was prepared to go to war if this was the only way to stop Communist power from spreading. He backed up his 'brinkmanship' policies with threats of 'massive retaliation'. If the United States or any of its allies were attacked anywhere, he warned, the Americans would strike back. If necessary they would drop nuclear bombs on the Soviet Union and China. By the mid-1950s the United States had a powerful force of nuclear bombers ready to do this. On airfields all round the world giant American planes were constantly on the alert, ready to take off against pre-selected targets at a moment's notice.

'Massive retaliation', 1950s style. An American B.52 bomber, range 14,500 kilometres

Despite the obvious risk that this threat of 'massive retaliation' might actually provoke a war, most Americans supported it at first. They knew that although the Russians had got H-bombs, they lacked the air power to hit the United States as hard as the United States could hit the Soviet Union. In 1957, however, a spectacular Russian achievement destroyed this confidence overnight.

On 4 October 1957 Russian scientists sent the *Sputnik*, the first earth satellite, roaring into space. The 'bleep-bleep' of its radio transmitter was soon being picked up all over an astonished world. The Russian achievement was so unexpected that some people simply refused to believe it. 'I shall believe it's true when the US navy says it's true!' said one stubborn American patriot to a television interviewer. Such doubters were soon convinced however. In the weeks which followed, the rocket which had blasted the *Sputnik* into orbit could easily be seen in the night skies as it too circled the earth.

It was the rocket which really worried the Americans. They realized that if it could carry a satellite into space it

'Massive retaliation', 1960s style. A Polaris missile-carrying nuclear submarine is launched in the United States

could also carry an H-bomb to its target; and it could do so faster and more accurately than any bomber. Overnight, it seemed, the Russians had overtaken the Americans in weapon technology and shifted the whole balance of world power in their favour.

American reaction was swift. They quickly speeded up their own rocket research programme. By the end of the 1950s a whole range of bomb-carrying rockets had been developed. The biggest of these were the I.C.B.M.s — the Inter-Continental Ballistic Missiles. A network of underground forts was built across the United States holding I.C.B.M.s with names like *Titan*, *Atlas* and *Minuteman*. Inside the forts the giant missiles waited, buried in steel and concrete containers to protect them from any surprise nuclear attack. If such an attack took place the rockets would rise to the surface and hurl their warheads on to targets continents away, on the far side of the earth. The whole process would take only minutes. Even deadlier was the Polaris underwater missile. This could be launched from nuclear-powered submarines cruising deep beneath the oceans.

The Beginnings of Co-existence

The hydrogen bomb and the practically unstoppable rockets to deliver it made leaders in both the United States and the Soviet Union think hard about their relations with one another. They came to recognize that with weapons like these the only possible result in any war would be unthinkable destruction for both of them. Cautiously, and without dropping their guards, they began to look for other ways of dealing with one another.

This search for a way to start 'thawing' the Cold War was made easier by the death of Stalin in 1953. After a struggle for power, Nikita Khrushchev came out on top in the Soviet Union. Khrushchev was a lively and seemingly jovial character, stout and bald-headed. Unlike the withdrawn and secretive Stalin, he loved to go travelling, mingling with the crowds and making rousing speeches. No one knew what he would do next. One minute he would be joking and roaring with laughter. The next he would lose his temper and start threatening to 'bury' the enemies of the Soviet Union.

Stalin had believed that, sooner or later, an all-out war with the American-led capitalist world was inevitable. Khrushchev was not so sure. He knew that it was difficult for capitalists and Communists to get on well together. They would only really agree, he said once, when 'shrimps learned to whistle'. But he also knew that in the age of the H-bomb there could be no winner in a war between the Soviet Union and the United States. In place of war Khrushchev suggested 'peaceful co-existence'. By this he meant that the Communist and non-Communist worlds should learn to live side by side. Like all Communists Khrushchev believed that the capitalist way of life would break down of its own accord one day. In this case, why risk a nuclear war against the Americans?

In 1955 President Eisenhower travelled to Geneva in Switzerland to meet Khrushchev and other Russian leaders. With the Russians smiling cheerfully for the cameramen and talking about co-existence, and Eisenhower saying things like 'It is not always necessary that people should think alike and believe alike before they can work together,' the atmosphere was very friendly. Little wonder that optimistic reporters started writing about 'the spirit of Geneva'.

The following year this development of friendlier relations suffered a setback. In October 1956 Russian tanks rolled into Hungary to crush the anti-communist rebellion there. In the same month Khrushchev threatened to launch nuclear missiles against America's allies, Britain and France, because they had attacked Egypt in a quarrel over the Suez Canal. But both these crises passed and as Eisenhower himself wrote later: 'the cordial atmosphere of the talks, dubbed the "Spirit of Geneva", never faded entirely. ... there began, between the United States and Russia, exchanges of trade exhibitions, scientists, musicians and other performers; visits were made by ... Russian leaders ... to the United States and returned by Vice President Nixon and my brother ... to the Soviet Union. These were small beginnings, but they could not have transpired in the atmosphere before Geneva.'

In September 1959 Eisenhower welcomed Khrushchev on a tour of the United States. Although no major new agreements were made, the two men agreed to meet again in Paris the following spring. The idea was to see if they could thrash out solutions to some of their differences, especially the still unsettled one of what to do about the future of a divided Germany.

Early in May 1960 Eisenhower, Khrushchev and other statesmen began to gather in Paris. But their 'Summit Conference' never even started. A Russian missile shot down an American aeroplane over the Soviet Union. The plane was a U.2, specially designed to take photographs of military targets from the edge of space.

Khrushchev accused the Americans of talking peace while planning for war and stormed off back to Russia. He appeared to be very angry. Secretly, however, he was perhaps rather pleased at having made the Americans look like hypocrites. Either way, the Paris 'Summit' of 1960 was over before it had even begun.

5 Co-existence and Conflict

Kennedy v. Khrushchev

Vienna 1961. Kennedy (right) and Khrushchev share a joke — but Kennedy returned to America believing that war could come at any time

In June 1961 two very different men met in Vienna, the capital city of Austria. One was the experienced sixty-seven-year-old Nikita Khrushchev. The other was a man young enough to be his son, the youthful looking Democrat, John F. Kennedy, who six months earlier had taken Eisenhower's place as President of the United States. In the closely fought Presidential Election of 1960 Kennedy had accused Eisenhower's administration of not competing hard enough with the Russians for world power and influence. He had promised that if he were elected he would remedy this.

Khrushchev set out to browbeat and intimidate Kennedy. He took a tough line from the start, especially about the future of Germany, demanding that the Americans should recognize the Communist government of East Germany and that they and the British and French should withdraw their troops from Berlin. He gave Kennedy six months to accept his demands and made dark hints about what the Soviet Union would do if the Americans refused.

Kennedy returned to the United States convinced that war could come at any time. On 25 July he announced a considerable strengthening of the American armed forces. He went on to spell out for the American people, and for Khrushchev, exactly where the United States stood on the Berlin question:

'West Berlin . . . is more than a show-case of liberty, a symbol, an island of freedom in a Communist sea. . . . above all, it has now become, as never before, the great testing place of Western courage. . . . We cannot and will not permit the Communists to drive us out of Berlin. . . . If we are not true to our word there, all that we have achieved in collective security, will mean nothing. And if there is one path above all others to war, it is the path of weakness and disunity. We shall seek peace, but we shall not surrender.'

Berlin and the Wall

It was a few minutes past midnight on Sunday, 13 August 1961. Through the silent streets of East Berlin armoured trucks rolled towards the border with the Western sectors of the divided city. When they reached the border police and soldiers jumped out and closed off all but twelve of the eighty crossing points. By morning tangled coils of barbed-wire had cut the city in two. Within days gangs of workmen started to replace the barbed-wire with a more permanent barrier of concrete blocks. The 'Berlin Wall' had been born.

To understand why all this happened it is necessary to go back a few years. All through the 1950s the two rival German governments set up after the Berlin blockade of 1949 (see pages 15–16) had criticized and quarrelled with one another. The leaders of the Federal German Republic (West Germany) wanted elections, which they believed they would win, to unite all Germany. The Communist leaders of the German Democratic Republic (East Germany) were opposed to this. They wanted East Germany to be recognized as a nation in its own right. The Russians supported them just as the Americans supported the West Germans.

Berlin occupied a special position at the very heart of this dispute. The West Germans and the Americans saw the city as the future capital of a united Germany. Until that day arrived they were determined to keep control of the former Western sectors and treat them as part of West Germany. The East Germans and the Russians objected to this. They saw West Berlin as an island of dangerous capitalist influence in their communist sea — a haven of 'counter revolutionary filth, spies, speculators... prostitutes and corrupted teddy boys' as the official Russian newspaper, *Pravda*, described it.

West Germany prospered in the 1950s. By 1961 her people were among the best off in the world. In East Germany people were less fortunate. Their standard of living was lower and their Communist rulers gave them less chance to speak their minds and to live as they wanted. Because of this many thousands of East Germans fled to the West. Many were skilled workers and professional people whom East Germany could ill afford to lose.

The favourite escape route was through West Berlin. Would-be escapers had simply to catch a train or a tram from East to West Berlin and then not make the return journey.

By July 1961 the number of people making such one-way trips to the West had risen to 10,000 a week. The whole economy of East Germany was threatening to collapse. It was to prevent this that the East Germans built the Berlin Wall.

In those August days in 1961 West Berliners gathered in thousands to watch the Wall rising. Many wanted the Americans and the British to send in tanks to destroy it. They were bitterly disappointed when this did not happen. 'When the Red Flag is flying over Buckingham Palace remember it all started... the day you let the Communists get away with

Looking across the Berlin Wall into East Berlin

sealing off East Berlin', was one West Berliner's angry comment to a reporter.

But neither Kennedy nor other Western leaders were prepared to risk war by tearing down the Wall. However, at the same time the President wanted to make it clear that, whatever happened on the border, the United States would not let the Communists take over West Berlin.

He ordered an armoured convoy of American troops to travel along the autobahn from West Germany through East German territory to Berlin. Khrushchev got the message. He dropped his demand that the whole German question must be settled by the end of the year and decided to settle for what he had won. The Berlin Wall was made stronger and East and West Berlin became, in effect, separate cities.

From the viewpoint of the East Germans the Berlin Wall achieved its purpose. The constant draining away of skilled manpower was stopped overnight and East German living standards slowly began to improve. But for millions of other people who had never seen Berlin the building of the Wall was not altogether a bad thing. By turning Berlin into two separate cities it removed a major cause of friction between the United States and the Soviet Union. One of the main flashpoints for a possible outbreak of war between the Communist and non-Communist worlds seemed to have been defused.

Foreign Aid and the Peace Corps

The Cold War was not always fought with concrete walls, barbed-wire fences and threats. Sometimes it was fought with food and tractors, medical supplies and water pumps, steel works and power stations.

American governments never forgot the lesson of the Marshall Plan. They knew that communism is often most attractive to people of countries where food is short and life is hard. From the 1950s onwards, therefore, they gave lots of aid to poor countries in Asia, Africa and Latin America. This 'foreign aid' became an important part of American plans to contain communism. Every year millions of dollars were spent on modernizing farms, constructing power stations and building roads in countries as far apart as Turkey and Colombia, Pakistan and Chile. The idea was to give poor people all over the world better lives, partly out of a genuine desire to help them but partly also to win new friends and supporters for the United States. To try to make sure that the countries aided stayed friendly, their rulers were often given money, and weapons such as tanks and jet aircraft, to help to keep them in power.

The Russians followed similar policies and for the same reasons. Although they spent far less than the Americans, under Khrushchev's leadership they were often very successful in 'buying' new friends in this way. In the late 1950s, for example, Khrushchev persuaded both Egypt, a key country in the Middle East, and Cuba, a key country in Latin America, to join the Russian camp by giving them large amounts of economic and military aid. You can read more about the aid to Cuba, and American reactions to it, in Chapter 6.

Foreign aid did not always take the shape of food,

Pakistan 1962. Peace Corps volunteers helping United Nations experts to advise a farmer on better ways to plough his land

machines or money. Sometimes human skills were sent, in the form of teachers and technical experts. Soon after Kennedy became President, he started a new scheme of this kind when he set up an organization called the Peace Corps.

The idea of the Peace Corps was to harness the enthusiasm and the technical skills of young Americans to help the people of 'underdeveloped' — that is poor — nations to help themselves. All members of the Peace Corps were volunteers, who agreed to work for two years as teachers and technicians in the poor countries of Asia, Africa and Latin America.

Some Americans disliked the scheme. They poured scorn on the idea of sending off immature and inexperienced young Americans to show the people of distant lands how to live. But others thought it both worthwhile and exciting. Whoever was right the Peace Corps achieved at least one thing — for a while it gave a human face to the bare financial statistics of American foreign aid.

6 America's Back Yard

The United States and Latin America

In the spring of 1958 President Eisenhower sent his Vice-President, Richard Nixon, on a goodwill tour of Latin America. Everywhere Nixon went he was met by angry crowds. In Peru he was mobbed. In Venezuela students pelted him with stones and eggs. At last, the tour was abandoned. The anti-Nixon demonstrations gave the people of the United States some idea of the anger and resentment that many Latin Americans felt towards them.

Latin America is the name given to the mainly Spanish-speaking countries which lie to the south of the United States. Ever since the early nineteenth century the United

Venezuela 1958. A crowd of anti-American students mobs Vice-President Nixon's car during his stormy tour of Latin America

States has taken a special interest in what goes on in these countries. They are her closest neighbours and so it is important to her safety to make sure that no foreign enemies gain influence there. In the past this has often meant that the rulers of these Latin American countries have been little more than American puppets. On top of this, much of their agriculture and industry has usually been American-controlled. A classic example was Cuba, where, up to the 1950s, the railways, the banks, the electricity industry and many of the biggest farms were all American-owned.

After the Second World War the United States took the lead in setting up the Organization of American States (O.A.S.). This was supposed to encourage the various countries of Latin America to help and co-operate with one another and with the United States. One of its aims was to improve living standards.

But hunger and distress continued to be widespread in Latin America. Wild extremes of poverty for the many and wealth for the few existed side by side in most countries. Oppressive governments controlled by the rich and backed by military force did little to improve the lives of the people.

Reformers accused the United States of keeping these cliques of wealthy tyrants in power. There was some truth in this. The American government usually seemed more concerned with suppressing communism in Latin America than with improving conditions of life there. In 1954, for example, the American secret service (the Central Intelligence Agency or C.I.A.) organized the overthrow of a reforming government in Guatemala. When its deposed President asked the United Nations to look into this the Americans used their Security Council veto to prevent an investigation.

In later years American governments went on interfering in Latin American affairs, sometimes openly, sometimes in more secret ways. In 1973, for example, American C.I.A. agents were behind an army rebellion in Chile in which another reforming government was overthrown because of its Communist sympathies.

Actions like these helped to explain why the North American 'yanquies' continued to be so disliked by many Latin Americans. All over the Continent, it seemed, the Americans were propping up corrupt and unpopular governments in order to fend off Communist take-overs.

There was another side to the picture, of course. President Kennedy, for example, set up the Alliance for Progress, which aimed to bring about improvements in the lives of the peoples of Latin America with financial backing from the United States. Despite this, many people saw little basic difference between the attitude of the United States towards Latin America and the attitude of the Soviet Union towards the Iron Curtain countries of Eastern Europe. Both seemed determined to protect their own interests by controlling their smaller neighbours in one way or another.

Revolution in Cuba

Cuba is a sugar-growing island only 145 kilometres off the coast of the United States (see map opposite). In the 1950s it was controlled by a small group of rich men led by a dictator named Fulgencio Batista. Batista was corrupt and cruel. While he piled up a personal fortune estimated at £100 million, the majority of Cubans lived in poverty, terrorized by his secret police. At last, in 1959, he was overthrown.

The man who drove out Batista was a bearded cigar-smoking young revolutionary named Fidel Castro. At first many Americans admired Castro. But then he started to make changes which alarmed them. Cuba's banks, railways, electricity and telephones were all American-owned. So was the all-important sugar industry from whose sales Cuba got most of the money she needed to pay for her imports from abroad. When Castro could not get the money he wanted to make reforms from anywhere else, he started to take over these businesses. The American government became worried. It seemed that Castro was introducing something very much like communism right on their doorstep.

President Eisenhower decided to force Castro to change his policies. His method was simple — the United States, Cuba's main customer, refused to buy any more of her sugar. However, the Soviet Union bought the sugar instead, so Eisenhower decided that the only thing to do was to get rid of Castro and put someone more co-operative in his place. Who this would be was undecided — so long as it was someone who would protect American interests!

Many Cubans who did not like Castro's revolutionary changes had taken refuge in the United States. Eisenhower had been told by the C.I.A. that most other Cubans were against Castro too so he decided to help the Cuban refugees to invade the island and overthrow the revolutionary leader. Secret training camps were set up and the Americans gave the refugees supplies of guns and ammunition.

In January 1961 Eisenhower's plan was inherited by the new President, John Kennedy. Kennedy gave the scheme the go-ahead. On 17 April 1961 1,400 anti-Castro Cubans land-ed on Cuba's south coast, at a place called the 'Bay of Pigs'.

The Bay of Pigs invasion was a disaster. The outdated

Cuban Missile Crisis, 1962

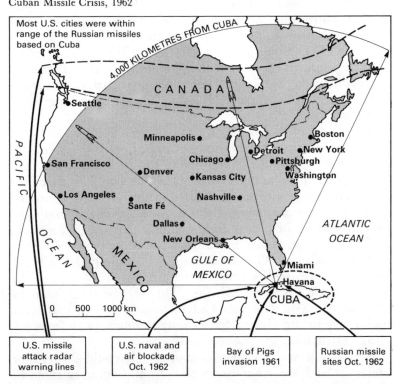

| U.S. missile attack radar warning lines | U.S. naval and air blockade Oct. 1962 | Bay of Pigs invasion 1961 | Russian missile sites Oct. 1962 |

45

Second World War bombers that the Americans had given the invaders were shot out of the skies by Castro's Russian-built jets. Their two main supply ships were sunk and within a couple of days 1,200 of the 1,400 invaders had been captured. Castro was triumphant.

The Bay of Pigs fiasco humiliated both the United States and its new President. Kennedy had unwisely agreed to a scheme that was now seen to have been doomed from the start by false information and poor planning. He promised himself that he would not make the same mistakes again.

The Cuban Crisis, 1962

As the light of dawn spread over Cuba on the morning of Sunday, 14 October 1962, a high-flying American U.2 crossed the island from north to south, taking photographs of the land many kilometres below with its long-range cameras. Within hours the photographs had been developed and printed and sent to intelligence experts to be studied. On the morning of Tuesday 16 October the photographs, together with the expert's reports on them, were handed to President Kennedy as he sat in his dressing-gown eating breakfast. The photographs showed Russian missile-launching sites being built in Cuba.

A build-up of Russian weapons had been going on in Cuba ever since the attack at the Bay of Pigs. Castro believed that it was only a matter of time before the Americans attacked him again so he asked Khrushchev for help. Khrushchev sent shiploads of weapons to Cuba — aircraft, tanks, torpedo boats, artillery and rifles. But he quickly realized that Castro's appeal for help gave him a chance that was too good to miss — an opportunity to outflank the Americans in the nuclear missile race. Bases in Cuba would bring practically the whole of the United States within reach of attack by medium-range Russian missiles. This can be seen from the map on page 45. The new Cuban missile sites placed every major city in the United States only minutes away from nuclear destruction.

Kennedy had a number of choices. He could do nothing and wait and see what happened. At the other extreme he could order the immediate destruction of the sites by either an air strike or a full-scale invasion. The danger of this second course was that the Russians might strike back against the United States, especially if some of their technicians manning the Cuban sites were killed. Then there was a third choice. Kennedy could order a blockade of Cuba to stop any more rockets from getting through and give Khrushchev a deadline to take the rockets already there back to the Soviet Union.

The President decided on the blockade. Orders were flashed to American ships to move into position around the coasts of Cuba. They were to stop any Russian ships carrying more rocket equipment to the island. Kennedy then contacted Khrushchev. He told the Russian leader that the missile sites must be destroyed and the rockets removed from Cuba. He warned that any rocket fired from Cuba would be regarded as a direct attack on the United States by the Soviet Union. As a final measure, he ordered 156 American nuclear missiles to be made ready to fire.

For ten days the world trembled on the edge of nuclear war. Other nations watched helplessly as the Americans and the Russians exchanged angry messages. Officials of the United Nations tried to act as go-betweens and keep both sides cool. Finally Khrushchev backed down. He ordered the launching sites to be destroyed and the rockets returned to the Soviet Union. In return Kennedy called off the blockade and promised that in future the United States would leave Cuba alone.

The most dangerous crisis of the Cold War was over.

7 The Vietnam Years

Revolution in Vietnam

Vietnam lies to the south of China. It is a long, narrow country, with bulges at each end where two broad river deltas push out into the China Sea. Most of its 32 million people live in these delta areas. Here, in small villages, they grow rice on flat and fertile fields surrounded by woodland.

Vietnam and the neighbouring countries of Laos and Cambodia (later known as Kampuchea), together make up Indo-China (see map on page 23). From the end of the nineteenth century until 1940 the whole area formed part of the French Overseas Empire. In 1940, however, Vietnam was taken over by the Japanese who continued to rule it until the Second World War ended in 1945.

During the Japanese occupation the Vietnamese people's desire for freedom from foreign rule grew very strong. A number of rival nationalist groups worked to achieve this. One of these groups was called the Viet Minh. It was founded in 1941 by a revolutionary leader named Ho Chi Minh.

Ho Chi Minh was a Communist, and he made sure that all the key positions in the Viet Minh were held by fellow Communists. In his own mind, his aims were clear. First, an independent Vietnam. Then, a Communist Vietnam.

By 1945 the Viet Minh already had guerrilla groups operating against the Japanese in the north of Vietnam. When the Japanese surrendered in August 1945 the Viet Minh took over the government of north Vietnam. But soon the French returned, anxious to reclaim their old colony. All attempts to reach agreement failed, and in December 1946 war broke out between the Viet Minh and the French.

At first the American government disapproved of the French attempt to crush the Viet Minh. They believed that all Ho Chi Minh wanted was to make Vietnam independent.

48

In 1949, however, after the Communist victory in neighbouring China, Ho stopped pretending. It became clear to the Americans that the Vietnamese leader was not just a nationalist — he was a Communist nationalist. Their attitude changed completely. They started looking for ways to contain communism in Vietnam.

By 1954 the American government was paying the French 500 million dollars a year — 80 per cent of the cost of their war against the Viet Minh. They also helped the French to set up a rival Vietnamese government in the south of the country. The Viet Minh had few supporters in the south and many of the people there welcomed the new government, especially when the Americans persuaded the French to promise to hand over full independence in the near future.

The war between Ho Chi Minh's forces and the French dragged on for eight long years. It ended with a final crushing defeat for the French army at the Battle of Dien Bien Phu in 1954. At a peace conference held in Geneva it was agreed that the French should leave Vietnam and that for the time being the country should be divided along a line drawn across its narrow waist.

In the North Ho Chi Minh's Communists took over the government. In the South non-Communist Vietnamese nationalists took over.

For most of the 1950s South Vietnam was ruled by Ngo Dinh Diem. Diem was ruthless, energetic and strongly anti-communist. He rooted out supporters of the Viet Minh and with American money and advice began to build up the economic and military strength of South Vietnam. By 1959 the Communists there — the Vietcong as they came to be known — had begun a war of sabotage and terrorism against Diem's government.

The Americans Get Involved

In October 1961 dozens of journalists turned up for a special display at an army base called Fort Bragg in the southern United States. The display was given by the Special Forces group of the American army, a crack unit skilled in the most modern methods of making war. President Kennedy had just approved an order to send a 400-man detachment from the unit to Vietnam to train the South Vietnamese army in its fight against the Communist guerrillas.

The unit showed its paces. A French reporter who had covered his own country's war in Vietnam ten years earlier said to an American friend: 'All this looks very impressive doesn't it?' His friend agreed. 'Funny', said the Frenchman, 'none of it worked for us when we tried it in 1951.'

The Americans had been sending supplies and equipment to South Vietnam all through the 1950s. But it was not until now, in 1961, that President Kennedy authorized the sending of American soldiers. Even then the soldiers were sent only to advise and support the South Vietnamese, not to fight.

One of Kennedy's advisers, the Under Secretary of State, George Ball, had been in Vietnam during the French war. Ball spoke out against sending the soldier advisers. He warned the President that the situation in Vietnam was so complicated and uncertain that if the United States sent soldiers of any kind there she might be dragged into a major war. The President just laughed. He had no intention of sending troops to fight in Vietnam. His generals had told him there would be no need to anyway. They assured him that with the right equipment and the right training the South Vietnamese soldiers would beat the Communists.

Yet within only a few years the United States had half a million fighting troops in Vietnam. The cause was simple. In the early 1960s it became clear that the South Vietnamese soldiers were losing the war. Ho Chi Minh was now sending men and equipment from the North to help the Vietcong guerrillas. The morale of the South Vietnamese soldiers was low, due partly to poor leadership and uncertainty about what they were fighting for, but mainly because, as the French reporter at Fort Bragg had foreseen, the Americans had trained and equipped the South Vietnamese soldiers for the wrong kind of war.

The war in Vietnam was one of ambushes and surprise attacks, not one of pitched battles. After an attack the Vietcong would melt away into the jungle or turn into peaceful villagers. Ordinary villagers would help and protect them, sometimes out of fear, sometimes out of sympathy for their

Vietnam 1966. A mother cradles her dead baby. Her husband, a Vietcong suspect, waits to see what his South Vietnamese capturers intend to do with him

cause. 'The people are the water, our armies the fish', as one of the Vietcong leaders put it. It needed something more than the latest tanks and other sophisticated military hardware to beat an enemy like this.

In 1964 the war became worse. In August Communist torpedo boats attacked American warships off the coast of North Vietnam. The Americans replied by sending planes from their aircraft carriers to bomb North Vietnamese naval bases. In retaliation the Vietcong raided one of the main American air bases in South Vietnam, penetrating its defences and tossing hand grenades amongst the parked planes.

By this time President Lyndon Johnson was making the decisions back in the United States. There had been a change of leadership in South Vietnam too. Ngo Dinh Diem had been overthrown by his generals in November 1963. Since then the government of South Vienam had been in chaos. Large areas of the country were now controlled by the Vietcong and it was clear that the government was close to collapse. Johnson was faced with the painful choice of letting the Communists take over or of sending American soldiers to join in the fighting in order to stop them.

Early in 1965 Johnson made his decision. Reluctantly, he ordered American combat troops to be sent into action in Vietnam. The United States was already too deeply involved, he felt, simply to withdraw. On top of this there was the 'domino theory' to consider. This had first been stated by President Eisenhower. The theory was that if one country in Asia — Vietnam, say — was allowed to fall under Communist control others would follow, nudged over one by one like a line of toppling dominoes.

All through the later 1960s a vicious war raged in Vietnam. Both the Russians and the Chinese sent equipment to Ho Chi Minh. Thousands of regular Communist troops marched south along secret jungle trails to give battle with the Americans. The Americans tried to stop them by laying waste vast areas of countryside. Many thousands of people, civilians and soldiers alike, were killed or maimed by terrible weapons such as explosive napalm fire-bombs. American bombers raided northern cities too, to try to force Ho Chi Minh to make peace. Instead, at the end of 1968, the Communists launched a massive new offensive, the 'Tet' offensive as it was called. They caught the Americans off guard. Although the Communists were finally beaten off with huge losses, they caused heavy damage. When pictures of this damage were shown on American television they helped to turn the Communist defeat into a psychological victory.

The American people were already uneasy about the war and its cruelty. Now, public opinion swung violently against it. People were tired of the endless destruction and killing in a country that seemed to have little to do with the United States. Was the war really necessary, they asked themselves? Was it just? They were worried too at the bitter divisions which the war was causing at home in the United States and about which you can read more further on in this chapter. More and more people came to believe that the President should do one thing above all others — get the United States 'out of the mess in Vietnam'.

The Americans Get Out

In March 1968 well over 500,000 Americans were fighting in Vietnam. Then the generals asked President Johnson for more. Another 200,000 more.

Johnson decided that this was impossible. He had already heard too many false promises of a quick military victory from these same generals. He knew now that in sending combat troops into Vietnam he had led his country into a trap that was destroying its good name in the world and undermining its unity at home. He decided to try to end it all. He ordered the bombing of Vietnam to be stopped and started to explore ways of negotiating peace with the Communists.

In January 1969 Johnson was replaced as President by Richard Nixon. Nixon had said during his election campaign that any man who couldn't end the war in Vietnam wasn't fit to be President. He soon made clear the first part of his plan to achieve this — 'Vietnamisation' of the war. This meant a gradual withdrawal of all American troops from the area, while leaving behind a Vietnamese force strong enough to continue to defend the South against the Communist attacks. Thus, while the Americans would still supply equipment to South Vietnam, the war would be fought only by Vietnamese against Vietnamese.

The second part of Nixon's plan was to persuade the Communists to sign a peace treaty. He sent his most trusted adviser on foreign affairs, Henry Kissinger, to secret talks with North Vietnamese leaders and with the Russians in Moscow. In return for a ceasefire he offered to withdraw all American troops from Vietnam within six months. When the Communists were slow to agree Nixon ordered the bombing of North Vietnam to begin again in order to 'persuade' them.

A peace agreement of a sort was finally patched together in January 1973. It was signed in Paris between the United

States and South Vietnam on one side and North Vietnam and representatives of the southern Vietcong on the other. It was agreed that there should be a ceasefire and that all American troops should be withdrawn.

By March 1973 all American troops had left Vietnam. But although the fighting eased off for a while, it never really stopped as it was supposed to. The real end of the war came finally in May 1975, when victorious Communist tanks rolled unopposed into Saigon, the capital city of South Vietnam. The Communists marked their victory by giving Saigon a new name. They called it Ho Chi Minh City.

As the final scenes were shown on television, a reporter asked various Americans what they thought of the matter. Most replied with expressions of anger, of shame and of waste. But one man sounded a note of hope — hope that the United States might learn something important from her experiences in Vietnam:

'There comes a time when each person suffers a staggering defeat in his own life. Vietnam is a defeat so major that we will never again...assume that we are somehow God's chosen nation. It ...will hopefully make us less arrogant, less nationalistic, more sensitive to the real concerns of other kinds of people.'

The Student Protest

'When I left home to return to school this autumn I was crying so hard my parents couldn't understand it. What they don't know is that I realised it was the last time I would ever be with them. Everything I said they looked down on, resented and ridiculed. I just don't have it in me to fight them. So I've left for good and I've left the kind of life they represent.'

The speaker was a teenage girl student in 1970. Her words reveal a division in American life at the end of the 1960s that was more worrying to many people than inflation, unemployment or any other problem. It was a division based on age, on what was sometimes called the 'generation gap'.

Kent State University 1970. Soldiers (in the background) fire tear gas bombs, as well as bullets, to break up the demonstrating students

Ironically, the discontent of young Americans showed itself first among those who were in many ways the most fortunate — the students of the universities and colleges.

The biggest cause of student unrest was the involvement of the United States in the Vietnam War. Students, like many adults, objected to the war because they thought it was cruel, unjust and unnecessary.

But there were other causes of conflict. The young criticized the older generation for their obsession with money and possessions, for their failure to solve national problems like poverty and racial injustice. The older generation in turn criticized the young for their ill-mannered behaviour and their appearance. An indignant housewife in 1970 said:

'My husband expects me to keep our house clean and myself neat ... I take pride in it, just as I take pride in his advancement in his work. It's what we got married for. Then I go into town and see these hippies, barefooted, filthy, elbowing me off the streets and using language I've never heard my husband speak. What am I to think? Have they taken over the world? Have we got to surrender to them?'

55

All over the country in the later 1960s there were continual protest meetings, sit-ins, and riots — against the Vietnam War, against political corruption, against racial and social injustice. One of President Nixon's chief advisers wrote to the President in 1970 that 'our young people, or at least a vast segment of them, believe they have no opportunity to communicate with government other than through violent confrontation.' The ugliest confrontation of all took place at Kent State University in Ohio in 1970. After riots in protest against the war in Vietnam, any further demonstrations were banned. When a group of about 1,000 students defied the ban, they were fired on by soldiers. A ten-second burst of rifle fire killed four students and wounded another ten.

The Kent State tragedy showed the frightening extent of the generation gap. 'After all, bullets against a gang of un-armed kids', said a student. 'Too much, man, too much!' But when another student asked a passer-by why he was holding up his hand with four fingers extended, he was told that it meant: 'This time we got four of you bastards; next time we'll get more'. 'The volley of gunfire served its purpose', said a writer to a local newspaper. 'It broke up a riot and I say the same method should be used again and again.'

Not all older Americans reacted as viciously and angrily as this to the killings. Most were shocked and many were ashamed. They agreed with the father of one of the dead students, a girl named Allison Krause, when he asked bitterly: 'Have we come to such a state in this country that a young girl has to be shot because she disagrees deeply with the actions of her government?'

In the 1970s conflict between the generations began to subside. Some of its causes were removed — the war in Vietnam was ended, for example, and with it the conscription of young men to go and fight there. Both sides too started showing a little more willingness to try to see the other's point of view. Although nobody realized it at the time, the Kent State tragedy proved to be the last of the confrontations between the generations.

8 An End to Cold War?

Co-existence After Cuba

'They talk about who lost and who won. Human reason won. Mankind won.' These words were spoken by the Russian leader Khrushchev after the Cuban Crisis of 1962. President Kennedy felt the same. For almost two weeks one word from either of them could have brought death to millions. To make such dangerous situations less likely they began to work harder to settle their differences. They recognized that whatever their differences the United States and the Soviet Union had one great interest in common — survival. It was thus not friendship that made the two countries try harder to understand one another; it was the fear of what might happen to them if they did not learn to do so.

Khrushchev gave one of the first signs of this new attitude when he dropped his earlier demands for changes in the position of West Berlin (see page 37). This removed a major cause of tension between the Soviet Union and the United States and opened the way for other agreements. In August 1963 the United States and the Soviet Union signed a treaty — the Test Ban Treaty — in which they agreed to stop testing nuclear explosives in the atmosphere or under water. At the same time a special telephone link was set up between Washington and Moscow. This 'hot line' meant that whenever a dangerous crisis arose in the future the leaders of the United States and the Soviet Union would be able to talk directly to one another at any time.

In 1963 Kennedy was murdered (see page 78) and a year later Khrushchev was removed from power. But the moves towards 'détente' — that is, a relaxation of tension — between the United States and the Soviet Union were continued by the new leaders in both countries. The 'hot line'

57

came in especially useful in 1967 when war flared up in the
Middle East between Israel and Egypt. The United States
was friendly towards Israel and the Soviet Union towards
Egypt. Both of them took great care, however, not to let
these friendships drag them into fighting one another. Even
the war in Vietnam, where the Russians provided Ho Chi
Minh with most of the equipment he used against the Americans, was not allowed to stop moves towards détente.

Not everyone welcomed these attempts to relax tension between the United States and the Soviet Union. In particular,
the Chinese leader, Mao Tse-tung, sneered at the Russian
leaders' policies and their fears of nuclear war. He called the
United States 'a paper tiger' and said that only cowards
would be afraid to fight her.

To him Khrushchev's talk of co-existence was a betrayal of
true communism. He accused the Russian leader of revision-
ism — that is, of altering some of communism's most important ideas. To Mao there seemed only one way to defeat
American capitalism — to fight it to the death, whatever the
cost. To Khrushchev talk of this kind was the raving of a
madman. He pointed out that the American 'paper tiger'
had 'nuclear teeth'.

Mao's answer to this was to give China nuclear teeth of
her own. When the Soviet Union refused to supply China
with nuclear weapons Mao ordered Chinese scientists to
make them. Just before China was ready to test her first
bomb Khrushchev and Kennedy signed the 1963 Test Ban
Treaty. This made Mao still more angry with Khrushchev,
for he thought the treaty was part of a plot to keep China
weak. His scientists continued their work and in October
1964 China exploded her first atomic bomb.

In the same month Khrushchev was dismissed as the leader of the Soviet Union. But the quarrel between China and the
Soviet Union went on. By the mid-1960s Mao and the new
Russian leaders were attacking each other's brand of communism angrily and openly. They also began to quarrel
about boundaries, with China claiming that large areas of
Russian land were rightfully hers.

In 1967 China exploded her first hydrogen bomb. The
Soviet Union grew steadily more afraid of her. So, too, did

China 1969. Communists against Communists. Chinese frontier guards defending Chinese territory against a possible Russian attack

other nations. Americans especially remembered Mao's threats and his reckless boasts about being unafraid of nuclear war. Many began to think that China was becoming more of a threat to their country's safety than the Soviet Union.

Kissinger and Nixon

In 1938 a shy, fifteen-year-old Jewish boy was forced to flee with his parents from the town in Germany where he had been born in order to escape imprisonment in one of Hitler's concentration camps. The family went to live in the United States where the boy got a job cleaning bristles in a shaving-brush factory. He was clever and hard working, however, and went on to become a brilliant student at Harvard University. Just over thirty years later he became possibly the most powerful Secretary of State the United States has ever had. His name was Henry Kissinger.

Some people believed that Kissinger's boyhood experiences in Germany played an important part in forming his ideas about the kind of world he wanted to shape as Secretary of State. One man who knew Kissinger said:

'I think he came out of it with a kind of burning need for

59

order. ... People in these experiences have a real memory of chaos, of violence and brutality, like the world is collapsing under them. ... Kissinger, more than most, would probably agree that disorder is worse than injustice.'

Kissinger's rise to importance began when Richard Nixon became President in 1969. He became Nixon's personal adviser in all America's dealings with the rest of the world. From then on he played a vital part in deciding American foreign policy, although it was not until 1973 that he officially became Secretary of State.

Both Nixon and Kissinger believed that the best hope for world stability was a situation where the power of the various stronger nations was evenly balanced. Nixon explained the idea like this:

'The only time in history that we have had any extended period of peace is when there was a balance of power. It is when one nation becomes infinitely more powerful than its potential competitor that the danger of war arises. So I believe in a world in which the United States is powerful. I think it will be a safer world and a better world if we have a strong, healthy United States, Europe, Soviet Union, China and Japan, each balancing the other.'

This idea of creating and maintaining a balance of power in the world was one of the two main themes of Nixon's foreign policy. The other was to extend the idea of détente.

Détente with the Soviet Union and China

On 22 May 1972 an American jet whistled in to land at Moscow Airport. From it stepped Richard Nixon, to be met by the President of the Soviet Union. It was the beginning of the first ever visit by an American president to Russia's capital city.

Nixon had come to Moscow to sign an agreement limiting the number of long-range nuclear weapons possessed by the United States and the Soviet Union. Talks to arrange this, the Strategic Arms Limitation Talks (S.A.L.T.), had begun in 1969. The aim was to save both countries from spending the vast amounts of money needed to go on building ever more advanced missiles and defences against them.

By 1972 agreement had been reached. The Russians were to be allowed 62 nuclear armed submarines and the Americans 44. On land, the Russians were to have 1,700 long-range missiles (I.C.B.M.s) and the Americans 1,054. The reason the Russians were allowed more missiles than the Americans was that the United States was felt to have advantages over the Soviet Union in other ways. One was the greater power and accuracy of her missiles. Another was her possession of bases close to the Russian borders. This 1972 S.A.L.T. agreement was to last until 1978, when both sides agreed to review the position.

Before Nixon left Moscow he signed other agreements with the Russian leaders — about trade, about exchanges of scientific and technical information and about co-operation in space. To round off the visit Nixon sat in a flower-decked room in Moscow's Kremlin palace and spoke live on television to the Russian people. The fact that a President of the United States could do this showed how relations between the superpower rivals had changed since the earlier and darker days of the Cold War.

By this time there had also been a decrease in hostility between the United States and China. The first moves had been made in 1970 when the Chinese government invited an American table tennis team to visit China. The American government took this as a hint that the Chinese leaders wanted to try to settle some of their differences with the United States.

The man behind the Chinese moves was Chou En-lai, China's Prime Minister and Mao Tse-tung's right-hand man. Chou believed that it was dangerous for China to continue to be so isolated on the international scene. Above all, she had to find some way to counterbalance the continuing hostility of the Soviet Union. He decided that one way to do this was to try to end the twenty-year-old feud with the United States.

Henry Kissinger flew to China for secret meetings with Chou and in the autumn of 1971 came the first big breakthrough. The American government agreed to Communist China joining the United Nations Organization, something

Détente. Mao Tse-tung greets President Nixon on his visit to China, 1972

they had blocked for years. A few months later President Nixon himself flew to China with Kissinger to meet Chou and Mao face to face.

Nixon's visit lasted in all for a week, and ended with a vast banquet. At the banquet Nixon told the Chinese leaders: 'We began our talks recognising that we have great differences, but we are determined that these differences will not prevent us from living in peace.'

These were just words. Nothing was said in the statement about concrete problems, like ending the war in Vietnam or about the United States continuing to support the rival Chinese government which Mao's old enemy, Chiang Kai-shek, was still leading on the island of Formosa (Taiwan). But at least the words were friendly words. That in itself was a considerable step forward.

Dangers in the Middle East

At the eastern end of the Mediterranean Sea lies the land of Palestine. In ancient times Palestine was the home of a people called the Jews. In later centuries many Jews left Palestine and scattered over the world to live in other lands. By the early years of the twentieth century fewer than one in ten of the people of Palestine were Jews. Most of the rest were Arabs, like the majority of other people in that part of the world.

The Jews who left were often badly treated in the lands where they settled. After the Second World War a flood of Jews from Europe tried to get into Palestine. Many were survivors of Hitler's death camps, who felt that they would only be safe in a land inhabited and ruled by other Jews. The Palestinian Arabs were alarmed at all these strangers pouring in. They feared that the land would soon be overrun. To them the newcomers were simply a lot of greedy foreigners, out to steal their homes and farms.

Soon there was fierce fighting. On 14 May 1948 the Jews proclaimed that Palestine now belonged to them. They set up a government and named their new country Israel.

The armies of neighbouring Arab countries like Egypt attacked immediately. They wanted to destroy Israel before it could grow strong. Israel only just managed to hang on, but in the end the Arabs were beaten and an armistice was signed. There was no lasting peace however. In 1956 and 1967 there was more fighting between Israel and her Arab neighbours. By now Israel was much stronger and each time the Arabs were heavily defeated and lost still more land.

The people who suffered most from these wars were the Arab peoples of Palestine. More than a million of them were driven from their homes to live in miserable refugee camps. Here they clung to the hope that one day Israel would be destroyed and that they would then be able to return to their old homes. Some of the camps became bases for Arab guerrilla fighters, who made surprise attacks on Jewish farms and settlements.

In October 1973 there was another full-scale war between Israel and her Arab neighbours. This time the Arab armies were more successful. But again the fighting settled nothing and it was followed by yet another uneasy ceasefire.

The Arab-Israel War of 1973 made the Americans take a fresh look at their policies in the Middle East. Up to this time they had favoured Israel, pouring money and arms into the country from its earliest years. One reason for this policy was the large number of Jewish Americans in the United States, many occupying positions of power and influence. Another was the desire of the United States government to have a strong ally in the Middle East. They wanted this as a kind of insurance against the area's rich supplies of oil ever falling under Communist control. Not surprisingly, the Russians had followed a counter policy of strengthening and supporting Egypt, the strongest of Israel's Arab neighbours.

The 1973 war worried both the Americans and the Russians. Both feared that one day an outbreak of fighting between Israel and her Arab neighbours might drag them unwillingly into war with one another. The Arab states had another powerful weapon too. After the 1973 war they agreed that until the Americans reduced their support for Israel, they would cut off supplies of their oil to the United States.

These were two of the reasons why, in November 1973, Henry Kissinger jetted to and fro round the world — to Moscow, to Israel, to Egypt — to thrash out the details of an agreement on the Middle East. At last he persuaded everyone involved to agree to certain main points. As a first step the fighting troops of the two sides — still angrily face to face after the October 1973 war — separated and let U.N. peacekeeping troops take up positions between them. This was done in the winter of 1973–4. As a next step, arrangements were made for further meetings between Arab and Israeli leaders to try to work out 'a final, just and lasting peace'.

For the rest of the 1970s American governments went on with this policy of trying to bring peace between Israel and Egypt. The two old enemies did settle some of their differences and became a little friendlier. But there were still many obstacles on the road to lasting peace between Israel and the Arab peoples generally. In particular, the central question of how to give the Palestinian Arab refugees a homeland again remained unsettled. Little wonder that these troubled lands

'...*hurry back, Kissinger, I'd like you to make a bit of peace around here*'

Washington D.C. 1973. President Nixon sends off Henry Kissinger on his Middle East peace mission. Why does the President want Kissinger 'to make a bit of peace around here'?

at the eastern end of the Mediterranean Sea continued to be one of the world's danger spots.

Isolation or Involvement?

Between the mid-1960s and the mid-1970s there were great changes in the attitudes of most Americans towards their country's rôle in the world.

After the Second World War Americans had come to believe that the United States had a duty to act as a sort of policeman, guarding the whole world against what they believed to be the evils of communism. This view was given its

65

most dramatic expression by John Kennedy when he stood on the steps of the Capitol building in Washington to be sworn in as President on a winter's day in 1961. In challenging, confident tones Kennedy declared: 'Let every nation know . . . that we shall pay any price, bear any burden, meet any hardship, support any friend, oppose any foe to assure the survival and success of liberty.'

These were intoxicating words. The listening crowd cheered and applauded wildly and all over the United States millions of people watching on television felt a thrill of pride in being Americans.

Twelve years later Richard Nixon stood on the same spot to be sworn in as President. But the tone of his comments on America's rôle in the world was very different from Kennedy's: 'We shall do our share in defending peace and freedom in the world,' he said, 'but we shall expect others to do their share. The time has passed when America will make . . . every other nation's future our responsibility . . .'.

One event provided the key to this more cautious and more self-centred attitude. That event was the Vietnam War.

Despite the deaths of more than 50,000 young Americans, American involvement in the war in Vietnam had ended in total failure. Nobody denied this. Nor did they deny the terrible suffering the Americans had helped to cause there. Their bombers had dropped over 7 million tonnes of bombs on Vietnam. Over a million Vietnamese had been killed and many more wounded. And what had been gained by it? Nothing. The deaths and the suffering had all been pointless.

The long agony of Vietnam had been shown on television all over the world and made many people see the Americans as cruel and bullying monsters. It had also caused bitter disagreements in the United States itself. There were those who supported the war and those who opposed it. Some of the most telling opposition came from soldiers returning home from service in Vietnam. 'We had to go to show we weren't cowards', they said. 'We went believing in the war. But we're back now. And we're telling you we've no business being there.'

After the bitterness and disappointment of the Vietnam War there were fears that the American people might return to their pre-Second World War policy of isolationism — that is, turn inward and try to ignore the problems of the rest of the world.

Kissinger and Nixon worked to prevent this new isolationism from developing. Even while they negotiated détente with the Soviet Union and China they insisted on the need for the United States to keep up her military strength and to continue to support her allies. Nixon warned: 'from a practical bargaining standpoint, the chances of conciliation are substantially reduced, if the man on the other side of the bargaining table thinks you're weaker than he is.'

But despite Nixon's words about the need for the United States to keep up her guard, in the mid-1970s some people feared that he and Kissinger were travelling too far and too fast along the road to détente with the Soviet Union and China. They feared that the United States was being lulled into a false sense of security. If this happened and the Americans dropped their defences, the Russians — or perhaps one day, the Chinese — might be tempted to strike. In 1979 the Russian take-over of Afghanistan seemed to confirm such fears. Détente, these critics pointed out, had not removed the differences and the rivalries between the Communist and non-Communist worlds. The different beliefs about the purpose of people's lives which had underlain the Cold War when it began in the 1940s were still there in the 1970s.

Optimists believed that as time passed these differences would become less marked. If all-out nuclear war could be avoided, they said, not merely co-existence but real friendship between the Communist and non-Communist worlds might eventually become possible. Others were less hopeful. They thought of the hundreds of missile-carrying submarines prowling beneath the oceans and of the thousands of land-based I.C.B.M.s on their carefully hidden launch pads. The chances were, they feared, that the day would come when someone, somewhere — either by accident, misunderstanding, recklessness or sheer madness — would give the order which would plunge mankind into nuclear war.

Only the future would show who was right.

Interlude — The Space Race

'I believe that this nation should commit itself to achieving the goal, before this decade is out, of landing a man on the moon and returning him safely to earth.'

The speaker was President Kennedy and the date was 25 May 1961. Even before his election Kennedy had promised to increase American activity in space. Now his proposal that the United States should send a man to the moon was eagerly welcomed by politicians and the American people. The first instalment of the estimated 24,000 million dollars that would be needed to pay for the project was quickly voted by Congress. Soon work was well under way on the Apollo programme, as the project was named.

The start of the Apollo programme was another move in the 'space race' between the United States and the Soviet Union. This had begun four years earlier, when the Russians had shocked the Americans by launching the first earth satellite, their Sputnik, into space (see page 32). Since then American scientists had worked hard to catch up and had successfully launched a number of satellites of their own. But early in 1961 the Russians forged ahead again. Only a month before Kennedy's speech they successfully sent the first man into space. This first Russian cosmonaut, Yuri Gagarin, orbited the earth before being brought back safely.

The costs of the space race were enormous. But there were two important reasons why both the Americans and the Russians were willing to meet them. First, there was the question of international prestige — of gaining the respect of the rest of the world by achieving something calling for such immense scientific and technical skill that it would be 'impressive to mankind' as Kennedy put it. Secondly, and even more important, there was the military side of the question. Both the Americans and the Russians felt that to let the other side

68

get too far ahead in space research and technology would endanger their security. Earth-orbiting satellites could be used to take spy photographs, for example. More frightening still, rockets capable of hurling people into space could also be used to hurl nuclear warheads against an enemy on earth.

So the space race went on, despite its cost.

Up to the mid-1960s the two sides were neck and neck, each matching the other's achievements. But then the Americans started to draw ahead. In November 1967 Saturn V, the rocket intended to carry their astronauts to the moon, made its first flight. Just over a year later, in December 1968, it carried three men into space on a mission which successfully circled the moon and then returned to earth. Finally, after two more test flights, all was ready for the mission to put men on the moon's surface — Apollo 11.

Apollo 11, like all the earlier Apollo missions, was to be launched from Cape Canaveral on the coast of Florida. Three men were selected as its crew. All were in their late thirties — Neil Armstrong 38, Edward 'Buzz' Aldrin 39 and Michael Collins 38. The first two would man the lunar module, the section of the spacecraft that would actually land on the moon's surface. Collins had the lonely job of circling the moon in the other section of the spacecraft, the command module, waiting for their return.

Launching preparations for Apollo 11 began four months before the flight, with the setting up and testing of its Saturn V rocket at Cape Canaveral. The final countdown started five days before blast off. At last, on 16 July 1969, burning 4½ tonnes of fuel a second, the huge 5,000 tonne rocket rose slowly from its launching pad on a roaring column of flame. Five days later millions of television viewers all over the world watched Neil Armstrong step down from the lunar module on to the surface of the moon.

Armstrong and Aldrin spent three hours loping about the moon's surface, collecting rock samples and setting up scientific instruments which would send information back to earth after they left. Then they rejoined Collins in the command module. Three days later they splashed down safely into the waters of the Pacific Ocean and were carried off by waiting helicopters to a heroes' welcome.

Apollo 11, 1969. Astronaut Aldrin plants an American flag on the moon

The first moon landing was a spectacular climax to man's exploration of space. But it did not mark its end. There were more flights to the moon, manned and un-manned. There were experiments like the Skylab flights in 1973 and 1974 aimed at testing the practicability of setting up manned space laboratories. Then there were journeys beyond the moon, to the planets. In 1976, for example, an un-manned American Mariner space vehicle landed safely on the surface of Mars and started to radio back pictures and other information to earth.

The American and Russian space programmes greatly increased man's knowledge — about electronics, the weather, the strengths of materials, the workings of the human body — the list was endless. But did such new knowledge justify the huge cost of the space race? Some argued that it did. They claimed that the benefits man would eventually get from his activities in space were beyond calculation. Others thought it was wrong, even immoral, to spend money so lavishly on space experiments in a world where millions of people were without enough food. Even those Americans who were proud of their country's space achievements felt a little uneasy. Looking at the problems of unemployment, poor housing and ill health that haunted large numbers of their fellow Americans, they occasionally wondered if some of the vast amounts spent on the space programme might not have been more profitably spent on such earthly problems.

9 Five Presidents

Harry S. Truman, 1945–1953

Harry Truman unexpectedly became President of the United States on the death of President Franklin D. Roosevelt in 1945. Nothing in Truman's earlier life seemed to have prepared him for such a powerful and responsible position. Born in Missouri in 1884, he tried his hand at various jobs before serving as an artilleryman in the First World War. After the war he opened a men's clothing shop and when this failed he found a new career in Missouri politics as a Democrat.

In 1934 Truman was elected to the United States Senate in Washington as a supporter of the 'New Deal' — the series of reforms introduced by President Roosevelt to help the United States out of the depression in employment and trade which hit the country in the early 1930s.

When Roosevelt chose Truman to be his vice-presidential running mate in the 1944 election, even Truman was surprised. It was a higher position than he had ever seriously thought of for himself. Little wonder that when Roosevelt died and Truman found himself President he felt that 'the moon, the stars and all the planets' had fallen on top of him.

Yet Truman was determined to live up to his new responsibilities. Abroad he came to be highly thought of by the allies of the United States. He was admired especially for the unhesitating, even aggressive, way in which he 'stood up to' Stalin, and for the generosity of the Marshall Plan. This side of his career is dealt with in more detail in Chapters 1–3.

At home in the United States Truman's reputation was not so high. He was accused of being cocky, quick tempered and lacking in judgement. At one time he seemed to make so many mistakes that his opponents adapted an old saying to describe him. Soon it was being repeated with amusement all over the country — 'To err is Truman'.

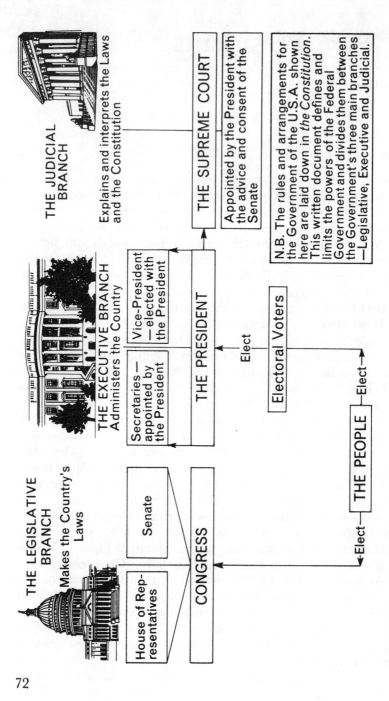

THE LEGISLATIVE BRANCH
Makes the Country's Laws

House of Rep-resentatives

Senate

CONGRESS

THE EXECUTIVE BRANCH
Administers the Country

Secretaries — appointed by the President

Vice-President — elected with the President

THE PRESIDENT

THE JUDICIAL BRANCH

Explains and interprets the Laws and the Constitution

THE SUPREME COURT

Appointed by the President with the advice and consent of the Senate

Electoral Voters

Elect

THE PEOPLE

Elect

Elect

N.B. The rules and arrangements for the Government of the U.S.A. shown here are laid down in *the Constitution*. This written document defines and limits the powers of the Federal Government and divides them between the Government's three main branches —Legislative, Executive and Judicial.

How the United States is governed

Truman's biggest problem in home affairs was to persuade Congress to pass the laws he thought the country needed. After the war he wanted to bring in more reforms in the tradition of the New Deal. But in the elections for Congress held in 1946 the Republican party got a majority of the places in both the Senate and the House of Representatives. The Republicans had always opposed Roosevelt's New Deal and now they also opposed what Truman called his 'Fair Deal'. The President found great difficulty in persuading Congress to pass any more laws of social reform. It turned down his plan to provide better medical services by means of a nationwide scheme of compulsory medical insurance. It rejected a scheme to ensure fairer treatment for American blacks. It even attacked some of the New Deal laws of earlier years. In 1947, for example, it passed a law called the Taft-Hartley Act which drastically reduced the rights which had been given to trade unions in the 1930s.

In 1948 there was a presidential election. Truman's chances of being elected to carry on looked hopeless. Even his own party, the Democrats, was not united in supporting him. Some thought that he was too much of a reformer, particularly in his plans to give blacks more rights. Others claimed that in foreign affairs he was not co-operating enough with the Russians. Both these groups put up presidential candidates of their own to oppose him. With the Democrats split three ways the Republicans grew certain of victory. All the experts agreed that Truman did not have a chance.

Truman refused to accept it. He boarded a train and set off to tour the country, making hundreds of informal, hard-hitting speeches wherever people gathered at a station to listen to him. He concentrated his attack on the Republican-controlled Congress which had turned down his Fair Deal reforms — the 'do-nothing' Congress, as he called it. He warned his listeners that this was a sign of what they could expect if they elected a Republican president. A 'do-nothing' government which would put all the gains of the New Deal years in danger.

Truman's arguments convinced millions of voters. People also admired his fighting spirit, his refusal to give in when everyone was saying he didn't have a chance. When election

President Truman 1948. The newspaper got the election result wrong

day arrived they gave him a comfortable majority to go back to the White House to carry on as President. It was probably the most satisfying moment of Truman's political life.

Truman served another full four years as President before retiring in 1953. He was much criticized towards the end of his second term, especially over his failure to end the Korean War (see page 26) and because some of the government officials he appointed were found to be dishonestly lining their own pockets with the taxpayers' money.

A famous saying about Truman summed up his career with the words: 'He was right on all the big things, wrong on all the little ones.' Truman's own summary was even simpler. He said that he would like to be remembered in words from the gravestone of a cowboy in a western cemetery: 'Here lies Harry Truman. He done his damnedest.'

Dwight D. Eisenhower, 1953–1961

By voting for Truman in the 1948 election the American people showed the politicians that they had not forgotten the unemployment and the hard times of the pre-war years. They wanted a president, and a government, who would take positive action to keep the country prosperous.

The lesson was not lost on the Republicans. When the time came for them to choose their candidate for the 1952 Presidential Election they passed over the leading figures in their party because they were all men who were known to be opposed to the Federal Government taking an active part in the nation's life. Instead, the Republicans chose as their candidate a popular general named Dwight D. Eisenhower.

Eisenhower, or 'Ike' as he was affectionately known, had been the Commander-in-Chief of the Allied forces in Western Europe during the Second World War. Despite this, he struck most people as being anything but warlike. On the contrary, compared with the fiery and quick tempered Truman, Eisenhower seemed tolerant and easygoing. This combination of friendly charm and his wartime reputation appealed to the voters. Eisenhower was helped too by the scandals and failures of the closing years of Truman's Presidency. On election day he won easily.

One of Eisenhower's first acts as President was to make peace in Korea. Then he turned his attention to home affairs. His approach to being President was very different from that

General Eisenhower (centre) during the Presidential Election Campaign of 1952

of Truman. Like other Republicans he wanted to reduce the rôle of the Federal Government in organizing and controlling the nation's life. To help him he appointed leading business-men to important positions in his government. One of them was the chief of the giant General Motors Corporation who became famous for saying: 'What is good for General Motors is good for America' — a statement often quoted against Eisenhower to try to prove that he ran the country in the in-terests of the big business firms.

Eisenhower had promised the voters that he would make drastic cuts in government spending. One way to do this, he thought, was to hand over to private firms jobs that might otherwise have been undertaken by the Federal Government — the building of new power dams, for example, and the de-velopment of atomic energy plants. In this way, he hoped to change the rôle of the Federal Government in the nation's life, 'trying to make it smaller, rather than bigger and finding things it can stop doing instead of seeking new things to do.'

There was an extreme example of this approach in 1955, when Dr. Jonas Salk discovered a vaccine to prevent the dreaded disease polio, which every year killed or crippled many thousands of young people. Eisenhower's Secretary of Health opposed the free distribution of Salk's vaccine by the government. This was because he was afraid, he said, that such actions might lead to government control of the medical profession 'by the back door'. As a result of attitudes like these there was little improvement in such social services as health, housing or schools during Eisenhower's years as President.

Even so, when Eisenhower gave up the Presidency the Federal Government was just as 'big' as it had been when he was elected. In some respects it was even bigger. By 1958, for example, it was spending six times as much money on trying to maintain the prosperity of American farmers by buying up their surplus crops as it had been doing in 1952. Eisenhower had also been forced to send troops to protect the rights of black children to attend schools which had previously been for whites only (see page 113).

But the biggest growth of federal activity arose out of the Cold War. It came from the vast sums of money that the government spent on weapons and weapons research during the 1950s. Although Eisenhower had been a fighting man himself, this worried him. When he retired in 1961 he made a speech in which he warned against the dangers of the increased power which all this spending on military equipment was giving to generals and weapon manufacturers — the 'military industrial complex' as he called them.

In the bitter years of American involvement in the Vietnam War (see pages 48–56) many people were to remember Eisenhower's warning and ask themselves a frightening question — was the real reason for the war to make jobs for generals and fat profits for armaments firms?

John F. Kennedy, 1961–1963

As the time approached for the Presidential Election of 1960 the United States was more powerful and more prosperous than at any time in her history. Her farming was the most productive in the world; her industrial output was reaching record heights; and her people enjoyed the highest standard of living the world had ever known.

Yet many Americans had an uneasy feeling that all was not well with their country. Although President Eisenhower continued to be personally well liked, there was a widespread feeling that in many ways the United States had come to a standstill under his leadership. There were problems about such things as unemployment, regional poverty and civil rights which nobody seemed interested in tackling. The United States, it seemed, had become smug and self-satisfied, a nation which had lost its drive.

The man the voters elected to do something about this was John F. Kennedy, the boyishly good-looking Democratic candidate. By a wafer-thin majority (unfairly obtained, according to his opponents) Kennedy became, at forty-three, the youngest President in the history of the United States.

Kennedy's background was very different from that of Truman and Eisenhower. The two earlier Presidents had both come from humble homes on the country's farmlands and each had risen to the Presidency almost by accident. Kennedy, by contrast, came from a very rich family. His

President Kennedy, 1961. Nearer the camera is Lyndon Johnson, the man who was to take over as President when Kennedy was killed

father ('that old crook Joe Kennedy' as Truman once described him) was a millionaire who had schemed for years and spent a fortune to try to ensure that his son became President.

John Kennedy's intelligence and personal charm made him a striking and popular President. He seemed to bring a youthful vigour and sense of purpose to the Presidency. He told the American people that they were facing a 'new frontier' and called upon them to join him in tackling its problems. 'My fellow Americans', he appealed to them in his inaugural speech 'ask not what your country can do for you, but what you can do for your country.'

Kennedy surrounded himself with a team of talented advisers and set out to make full use of the powers of the

Presidency. In home affairs he had many difficulties to over-come. He found himself facing strong opposition in Congress, both from Republicans and old-fashioned southern Demo-crats. As a result he was unable to bring in some of the laws he wanted. A scheme for the government to help to pay for medical care for old people, for example, was rejected by Congress. So too was a scheme to provide money to improve the nation's schools.

Despite such setbacks, in other directions the Kennedy government soon had a number of important achievements to its credit. Minimum wages were increased in many jobs; more government money was given for housing schemes in poor areas; and steps were taken to work out special pro-grammes of help for regions of the country where there was mass unemployment.

This last measure was an attempt by Kennedy to tackle one of the most worrying features of American life in the 1960s. This was the fact that, despite the general prosperity, millions of people were unable to find jobs. Kennedy particu-larly wanted to help the people of the once prosperous coal mining area of Appalachia whose poverty he had seen for himself during the 1960 Election Campaign. (You can read more about Appalachia and its problems in Chapter 11.)

But perhaps Kennedy's most urgent problem was that of civil rights. All through the 1950s black Americans had con-tinued to struggle to get fair treatment. When Kennedy be-came President they got more support from the Federal Gov-ernment. In 1962, for example, the President sent troops to enforce the right of a young black to enrol at a university in a southern state. But this was only a beginning. By 1963 Ken-nedy had worked out a detailed scheme to try to ensure that all Americans, whatever their race, would receive just and equal treatment and had sent it to Congress to be made law.

Kennedy himself never saw this happen. His reforming policies had earned him the hatred of many fanatics and in November 1963 he was shot and killed while driving through the streets of the city of Dallas in Texas.

The murder of President Kennedy shocked not just the United States but the whole world. His combination of ideal-ism and determination, of intelligence and warmth, had

caused the appeal of his personality to be felt far beyond the
frontiers of the United States. For millions of people speaking
dozens of languages it was as if a symbol of hope for the future had died on the streets of Dallas. 'John Kennedy's death
has greater pathos because he had barely begun', wrote a
close friend. 'He had so much to do, so much to give — to
his family, his nation, his world. His was a life of incalculable
and now of unfulfilled possibility.'

In the years to come people would sometimes see John
Kennedy in a less favourable light. They would learn how
his father's money had been used to buy favourable public-
ity, and sometimes votes, for him. They would remember too
that it was he who sent the first American troops to fight in
Vietnam. Nevertheless he remains for many the most attractive political figure of his time.

Lyndon B. Johnson, 1963–1969

The Presidential jet *Air Force One* stood parked on Love
Airfield in Dallas. A few hours earlier it had landed with
President and Mrs. Kennedy on board. Now the President
was dead.

At two o'clock a heavily escorted car drove up to the jet.
Out of the car and on to the plane stepped Kennedy's Vice-
President, Lyndon B. Johnson. In the plane's gold-
upholstered conference room Johnson took the oath of office
as President. Minutes later the jet roared into the sky and
headed back towards Washington.

Johnson was a fifty-five-year-old Texan — tough, vain and
shrewd. He loved political power and after nearly thirty
years as a professional politician he knew just about all there
was to know about getting it and using it. Yet for all this, he
was something of an idealist. He once summed up his political views in these words:

'I get more satisfaction out of doing things for people than
anything else. I like to think I'm a liberal without being a
radical. To put it another way, I always want to keep moving — but not with both feet off the ground at the same
time.'

Johnson certainly 'kept moving' when he became President. First he persuaded Congress to pass Kennedy's Civil Rights Act. Johnson deserved a lot of personal credit for this. He had little of Kennedy's charm or personal magnetism, but he knew far more than Kennedy about how to get Congress to do what he wanted. For many years he had been a leading figure there himself and this gave him the influence and the knowledge to persuade Congressmen whom Kennedy had been unable to budge. His Vice-President, Hubert Humphrey, said:

'Lyndon Johnson was a master at dealing with Congress. None better. That was [his] great talent. ... He not only said what he wanted, he went out and got it. And he maybe broke a back here and there, or twisted an arm out of its socket, but he always brought you over to the clinic and had you repaired.'

Johnson had Kennedy's other problems to tackle, as well as civil rights. In particular there were the continuing twin problems of large-scale unemployment and poverty. To many Americans it seemed intolerable that this kind of distress should be allowed to continue in their country, the richest in the world. A feeling that change was needed was one of the reasons why, in the Presidential Election of 1964, they re-elected Lyndon Johnson as their President by the largest majority ever recorded in the history of the United States.

When he was sworn in as President in January 1965 Johnson promised to carry on a 'war on poverty' and to create in the United States what he called 'The Great Society', a society based upon principles of justice and humanity. There seemed a good chance that he would be able to do this. He had the support of the people and the political skill to get Congress to pass the laws that were needed. It seemed that the United States was about to take a great step forward.

But tragedy lay ahead, for Johnson and for the United States. Despite his other political skills, Johnson never really understood foreign affairs. In the 1964 Election he had promised to make sure that the United States did not get any more involved in the war in Vietnam (see page 51). But instead he took the advice of his generals and involved her more deeply, stepping up or 'escalating' the war and sending in bombers and more troops in a vain attempt to force the Vietcong to make peace.

As the cruel and pointless struggle in Vietnam dragged on Johnson saw all his hopes of creating 'The Great Society' fade and disappear. The cost of the war forced him to give up many of his plans for social reform. There were riots and protests all over the country, in city after city — against the war, against poverty, against continuing racial injustice. By 1968 the nation was so deeply divided that Johnson decided that it was hopeless even to try to get re-elected and announced his intention to retire.

'He will be remembered', wrote one observer, 'for the sorrows that befell the United States during his Presidency. The monument to his great talents is inscribed with the names of the dead in the war abroad and the insurrections at home.'

Richard M. Nixon, 1969–1974

The man who was elected to replace President Johnson was the Republican Richard Nixon, a lawyer from California. Nixon had been Eisenhower's Vice-President in the 1950s and was the man who had been narrowly defeated by John Kennedy in the Presidential Election of 1960.

Only a few months after Nixon took office the United States showed its immense industrial and scientific power by landing two men on the moon (see page 69). But at home the new President faced disturbing problems. As the 1960s came to an end the American people were disillusioned and bitterly divided. There was hostility between blacks and whites, between young people and their elders, between those who were for the Vietnam War and those who were against it. There was a cynical lack of faith in the government — a 'credibility gap' as it was called — because of the difference between what the politicians said was the truth, and what people could see was the truth. There was a cost of living problem, an unemployment problem, a crime problem. 'It seems to me a staggering lot of questions for one society to have to tackle at one time', commented a historian.

One of Nixon's strongest personal beliefs was that victory

over hardship comes to people who are prepared to help themselves. For this reason he was much less interested than Kennedy and Johnson had been in taking government action to help the poor. 'The average American is just like a child in the family', said Nixon. 'You give him some responsibility and he is going to amount to something. If, on the other hand, you make him completely dependent and pamper him ... you are going to make him soft, spoiled and eventually a very weak individual.'

Nixon believed that the government was spending more than enough money already on social services and welfare schemes. What was needed now was efficient administration of the government's spending to make sure that the tax-payers' money was not wasted.

In November 1972 the American voters re-elected Nixon as their President. His majority was a large one. One of the main reasons for this was that by this time Nixon seemed close to getting the United States out of the war in Vietnam, a war which many Americans believed to be at the root of their country's worst difficulties. In January 1973 a ceasefire was finally signed and arrangements were made for all American fighting men to withdraw from Vietnam. It was Nixon's moment of greatest triumph.

But storm clouds were gathering. Six months earlier five men had been arrested while breaking into the Democratic Party's headquarters in the Watergate office block in Washington. It was now revealed that the burglars had been paid to steal information to discredit the Democrats in order to ensure Nixon's re-election.

The Senate set up a special committee to investigate the Watergate affair. Its meetings were broadcast live on television. Day by day they revealed to the American people a network of bribery, lies and dishonesty at the very heart of the nation's government.

Nixon vowed repeatedly that he had known nothing about the Watergate break-in. But as the investigations went on fewer and fewer people believed him. By the end of the year demands were growing that he should be put on trial — impeached — for misusing the powers of the Presidency. The end came in August 1974. To avoid the impeachment and possible imprisonment which now seemed certain, Richard Nixon resigned his position as President of the United States — the first man in the country's history ever to do so.

To many people at home and abroad the Watergate affair seemed to provide damning evidence that the American political system had gone rotten at the core. But it was parts of that very system — the newspapers, the law courts, the Congress — which brought the misdeeds of the President and his advisers to light. They showed that not even the highest in the land were above the law.

Ironically, it was Nixon himself who perhaps best summed up this aspect of the Watergate affair. Shortly before his resignation he said:

'Some people will say that Watergate demonstrates the bankruptcy of the American system, ... I believe precisely the opposite is true. Watergate represented a series of illegal acts. It was the system that brought these facts to life and that will bring those guilty to justice.'

Postscript, 1980

On 9 August 1974, a few hours after a helicopter carrying Richard Nixon rose clattering off the White House lawn, his Vice-President, Gerald Ford, was sworn in as President.

Politically, Ford was a more honest, more straightforward version of Nixon himself — a cautious, conservative Republican. 'If I can be remembered for restoring public confidence in the Presidency, for achieving decent results domestically, as well as internationally, I think that's what I'd like on my tombstone', he said later.

Ford achieved what he set out to do. For two and a half years he gave the American people a period of calm in which they had time to settle down and take stock of their position. Not surprisingly, they decided that what the country needed above all was a return to honesty and open dealing in government. They decided that Ford was not the man to give them this. Despite his personal honesty, he was surrounded by too many of Nixon's old cronies. When the Presidential Election of 1976 came round the voters elected a man whose

Four presidents 1981. President Reagan (second from left) raising his glass at a White House reception to his predecessors, the former Presidents (left to right) Nixon, Ford and Carter

election campaign was based largely on the one simple statement: 'I will never lie to you.' This was Jimmy Carter, the Democratic Governor of the state of Georgia.

Carter's Presidency was not a happy one, for himself or for the United States. Four years later in the Presidential Election of 1980, he was crushingly defeated. The basic reason for this was that too many of his policies ended in failure, both abroad and at home. The voters were particularly angry at his failure to stop steep increases in both prices and unemployment. Fairly or unfairly, they became convinced that Carter was incompetent and simply not worth re-electing. 'A lot of people went into the voting booths and said "To hell with it, I'm not going to reward four years of failure".' commented one observer. They voted instead for Carter's opponent, the sixty-nine-year-old former film actor, Ronald Reagan.

The future would show how wise, or how mistaken, their choice had been.

10 Industry, Employment and Trade

An Industrial Giant

The United States was the only great power to come out of the Second World War stronger economically than she went into it. Her cities and farmlands, her oil wells and mines were all undamaged. She had many new factories, built during the war to turn out weapons and equipment and available afterwards to make peacetime goods. The result was that between 1939 and 1947 American industrial output trebled and the number of jobs in industry increased by more than half (52 per cent).

After 1947 old jobs disappeared, new ones emerged. A whole range of new, chemically-based plastic materials came into use. There was an apparently endless demand for new products, like miniaturized electronic components to go into missiles for the government, computers for the businessman and televison sets for the ordinary person in the street. Industry changed and grew, with output reaching new records.

A major reason for the prosperity of industry was the rising standard of living in the United States. When the fighting ended in 1945 people were hungry for cars, refrigerators, television sets and other durable consumer goods. Their sales kept American industry growing for the next thirty years or more.

Another important factor in the growth of American industry was the massive amounts of military and other equipment that the government ordered from private industry all through these years. At the peak of the American space programme of the 1960s, for example, more than 20,000 industrial firms were working on the project. They ranged from small, specialized concerns making such things as antennae, to the giant aircraft companies which made the actual space

1. Impala Convertible

2. Parkwood 9-Passenger Station Wagon

3. Impala Sport Sedan

Chevy's Jet-smooth ride paves the way to out-of-the-way places!

Take to the hills or head down some winding backwoods trail in a Jet-smooth Chevy! It's *made* for that kind of travel. With big Full Coil springs that calm jittery roads. With a deep-well trunk that lets you take along a mountain of gear and equipment. And with Chevrolet's ever-famous dependability for added peace of mind. Try one, for sure. . . . Chevrolet Division of General Motors, Detroit 2, Michigan.

1. *Impala Convertible.* Homebodies who drive this one will never be the same again!

2. *Parkwood 9-Passenger Station Wagon.* With a concealed compartment for stowing valuables under the rear-facing third seat.

3. *Impala Sport Sedan.* You won't find more luxury for the money in anybody's lineup!

CHEVROLET

'Most Americans enjoyed a time of unbroken prosperity from the 1940s to the 1970s'. Car advert, 1961

vehicles and rockets. The contracts ran into hundreds of millions of dollars and provided jobs for nearly half a million people.

The growth of industry meant that most Americans enjoyed a time of unbroken prosperity from the 1940s to the 1970s. In the middle of the 1970s the United States had a population of 210 million people. This was 5 per cent of the world's total population — but the 5 per cent was producing 25 per cent of the world's total economic wealth. It was using a good deal of it too. At this time, for example, 33 per cent of the oil produced in the world was being consumed in the United States.

The United States in the 1970s was thus an industrial giant, overshadowing every other nation on earth. Her people owned half of the world's telephones, half of its radios, half of its cars, and two-thirds of its televison sets. Little wonder that the annual income of the largest American manufacturing firm, the General Motors Corporation, was larger than that of the government of France!

The Bigness of Business

Calvin Coolidge, a President of the United States in the 1920s, once said: 'the chief business of America is business.' This was still true fifty years later. It was estimated that there were by then about 12 million businesses of one kind or another in the United States, ranging from small, one-man concerns to giant companies with thousands of employees. None were government-owned, for American economic life is based upon the capitalist, or free-enterprise system. Under this system individuals and corporations (as Americans call industrial and business companies) compete against one another to get all the customers and all the profits they can. About 75 per cent of America's wealth is produced like this, the remainder coming from government activities.

By the 1970s, however, some people were beginning to wonder how genuine a lot of this supposed competition was. At this time two-thirds of the manufacturing capacity of the United States was owned by 200 corporations. A generation earlier that two-thirds share had been spread between 1,000

'The business of America is business'. Offices, hotels, department stores in the central business district of the city of Philadelphia

corporations and at the start of the century between 2,000. In other words, all through the twentieth century big American business companies have got steadily bigger.

Some of the giant corporations have grown naturally, by producing and selling more and more of the products they know best. But others have grown as a result of what has been called 'company eating'. This is when big corporations buy control of, or take over, smaller and less wealthy firms. In 1969 alone, some 4,550 previously independent American firms were swallowed up in this way.

A good example of a 'company eater' is the United States' largest firm, the General Motors Corporation. General Motors' main business is making motor cars, or automobiles, as Americans call them. Over the years General Motors swallowed up, one by one, a string of famous and previously independent automobile manufacturers — Buick, Oldsmobile, Cadillac. But company eaters don't stop at taking over firms in their own main line of business. They buy up other kinds too. General Motors, for example, is America's largest producer of washing machines and colour television sets, as well as of cars.

The ownership of the giant corporations is shared out amongst millions of people, for buying shares in successful companies is widespread in the United States, even among people who are not especially wealthy. In 1950 it was estimated that one American adult in every sixteen owned shares of one kind or another. By 1970 the figure had risen to one in every four, making a total of 30 million shareholders.

But although ownership of the corporations is widespread, control of them is not. Their business policies and day-to-day running are usually in the hands of a small number of top managers. The immense power of these 'organization men' over the nation's economic life, and thus over the jobs and well-being of millions of people, is one thing that worries people about the giant corporations. Another worry is the way in which the giants seem to be endangering genuinely free competition in industry.

Most Americans are great believers in competition. They believe that if manufacturers have to compete for customers against other manufacturers, people will get the best possible product at the lowest possible price. But fewer companies means less competition. People suspect that big firms in the same line of business are sometimes working together secretly to keep prices artificially high.

Defenders of the big corporations claim that most such criticisms are exaggerated. They point out that without the giant corporations American prosperity would collapse. Their very size is what makes it possible for American industry to produce goods that are cheap enough for the great mass of the people to afford. The defenders of the corporations claim too that only such huge and wealthy organizations can afford all the costly research work that is vital for modern industry to remain up-to-date and efficient.

The Worker and the Unions

In 1960 there were almost 67 million jobs in the United States, compared with just under 54 million in 1945. By 1970 there were 80 million and by 1974 85 million.

In the 1970s about half of these jobs were filled by 'white collar' workers — office staff, sales people, technicians and

Industry, Employment and Trade

professionals like doctors and lawyers. Another third were what Americans called 'blue collar' or 'hard hat' jobs — factory operatives, labourers, construction workers. The remainder were jobs in other service industries such as transport (about one-eighth) or in farming (about one twenty-seventh).

These figures show something more than a general increase in employment in the United States since the Second World War. They also show considerable changes in patterns of employment — that is, in the kinds of jobs by which Americans earn their living. The big shift has been from jobs concerned with producing goods (down from 49.8 per cent of the total labour force in 1950 to 39.5 per cent in 1970), to jobs that are connected with providing services (up from 50.2 per cent in 1950 to 60.5 per cent in 1970).

For the great majority of American workers the years since 1945 have been good ones, whatever their jobs. Their incomes have risen steadily. Between 1945 and 1965 the real value (that is, the buying power) of the average American worker's pay cheque rose by about half. One reason for this was the country's general prosperity during these years. Another was the increase in the productivity and efficiency of industry. Yet another factor was the power of the trade union movements — 'organized labour', as it is known in the United States. In 1940 fewer than 9 million Americans belonged to unions; by 1955 nearly 15 million were members and by 1975 about 20 million.

Large though this 1975 figure was, it still meant that for every American worker who belonged to a trade union, there were three others who did not. This is a smaller proportion than in many other industrialized countries. Despite this, the unions had considerable political influence. Politicians were always ready to pay attention to their views in order to try to get the votes of their members in elections.

Most union leaders were honest and dedicated men, who worked hard for the good of their members. But there were exceptions, those whose corruption and dishonesty gave the union movement as a whole a bad name. To try to improve things, in 1959 Congress passed a law called the Landrum-Griffin Act. This made it compulsory for union officials to be chosen by a secret ballot and brought in tighter controls over the handling of union money.

A problem that has troubled American industry less since 1945 than many other industrialized countries is that of strikes. One reason for this is that American workers usually seem more prepared than those in most other industrial countries to co-operate and work in partnership with the managers and owners of industry. Another reason is a law called the Taft-Hartley Act which was passed by Congress in 1947. Amongst other things the Taft-Hartley Act gave the President the power to order a union to postpone any strike which he believed was a serious threat to the nation's safety or prosperity. The ban was legal for eighty days, during which time it was the job of all concerned to find a solution to the problems behind the strike. This 'cooling off' procedure proved very useful. Between them, President Truman and President Eisenhower used it no less than seventeen times, and averted a number of potentially damaging strikes.

The Government and the Economy

Every American President since 1945 has believed that one of his main jobs is to help to keep the country at work and prospering. In general they have succeeded, but there have been two persistent problems. One is inflation — that is, a situation where prices rise so much that money begins to lose its value. The other is unemployment.

These twin problems plagued American governments from the 1940s through to the 1970s. The difficulty was that whatever the government did to control one seemed to encourage the other. If it encouraged spending, prices rose. If it cut back on spending, people were thrown out of work. Unemployment rose and fell in waves. In 1958 it reached a peak of 5.2 million, in 1961 5.3 million, in 1976 8 million.

In the middle 1960s inflation was fuelled by the huge amounts the government was spending on the Vietnam War. When President Nixon set out to bring the war to an end, he hoped that amongst other things this would help to stop inflation. But all that happened was that with the government ordering fewer aircraft, tanks and other kinds of military

A Russian cartoon attacks the Americans for not solving the problem of poverty. 'Get away, you're spoiling the whole show', the businessman tells the five million unemployed

equipment for Vietnam, firms that depended on such work began to lay off workers. Unemployment grew while inflation went on. The crisis came to a head in August 1971. In the middle of the month President Nixon imposed a complete ban on all wage and price rises.

Although Nixon's ban was relaxed later, from this time on-wards the Federal Government kept a variety of controls over wages and prices. The old political dispute between Democrats and Republicans, about whether the government should play a major part in the nation's economic life, seemed dead at last. The question, now and for the future, was exactly how big that part should be.

Foreign Trade

A hundred years ago the United States was a nation whose foreign trade consisted mainly of shipping out food crops and raw materials and shipping in manufactured goods. In the twentieth century, however, the United States itself became the world's leading manufacturing nation. As well as continuing to export food and other farm products, she came to export vast quantities of manufactured goods too. These two things together — the sale overseas of both food and manufactured goods — gave the United States a very favourable 'balance of trade' with the rest of the world. That is, she was always in a position of selling more to other countries than she needed to buy from them. This meant that her trading partners had to make up the difference in cash.

Over the years this foreign money grew into a vast treasure. Much of it was eventually turned into gold bars which were kept safe in the underground strongrooms of a heavily guarded government fortress called Fort Knox. The American dollar came to be looked upon as the strongest and

New York 1962. Checking part of America's stock of gold bars in a Federal bank

safest form of money in the world. It was the one against which the value of every other currency — the British pound, the German mark, the French franc, the Japanese yen — was measured.

From 1918 onwards there was a permanent 'dollar gap' in trade between the United States and Europe. Try as they might, other countries just could not sell enough to the United States to pay for their imports from her. During the Second World War this gap was bridged by President Roosevelt's Lend-Lease Plan. Under Lend-Lease the United States practically gave the nations fighting Nazi Germany the goods they needed to carry on the struggle. After the war, with Europe in ruins, the dollar gap grew even wider. This time it was bridged by the Marshall Plan, which is described in Chapter 2. The United States gave similar aid to Japan and to other countries.

In 1950 it looked as if the dollar gap could never be closed. But by the 1960s the situation had changed. The war-ruined trading partners of the United States had built up their industries again. They were making determined and successful attempts to sell their goods to American customers. German cars, Japanese cameras, British textiles — more and more of them appeared in American shops and showrooms. The United States' favourable balance of trade began to shrink and in 1971 a new kind of dollar gap appeared. For the first time in her history the United States bought more from other countries than she sold to them.

This unfavourable trade balance, together with the inflation described earlier in this chapter, caused the dollar to fall in value in the early 1970s. But the underlying strength of the American economy remained. In 1971, for example, the total value of all the goods of all kinds produced in the United States rose above 1 trillion (a million million) dollars for the first time. This amounted to one-third of all the wealth produced in the whole of the world in that year.

A fact like this suggested that despite its economic problems it was much too early to start counting out the United States as the world's leading industrial and trading nation.

11 Places and Problems

Appalachia

Appalachia is the name of a region of the eastern United States. But by the 1960s the word had an additional meaning — poverty.

Appalachia gets its name from a series of mountain ranges and plateaux called the Appalachians, which run most of the length of the United States some 300 kilometres inland from the east coast (see map on page vi). Appalachia is the central part of this system. It is a maze of valleys and forested hills, with twisting roads and few open spaces. The area as a whole comes under seven different state governments.

For many years the people of Appalachia were mainly farmers, scratching a bare living from tiny fields on the hillsides

Appalachian poverty. Bare shelves, bare floors and peeling walls in the home of a striking miner

and in the valley bottoms. Then, in the closing years of the nineteenth century, coal mining came to the valleys. Appalachian coal was easy to get at. Instead of having to sink shafts and tunnel underground for it, the mining companies could often extract the coal by open-cast methods. That is, they could get at the shallow underground seams by simply tearing away the top soil which covered them. When the coal had been taken the mining companies moved on, leaving behind a ruined and useless landscape.

An unusual feature of the development of mining in Appalachia was that few towns grew up there. Although a lot of people live in the area, most were scattered about the hills in lonely cabins. If a man wanted to work as a coal miner he had to be prepared to move into one of the camps set up by the mining companies.

Despite such drawbacks, mining meant jobs and money and the people of Appalachia had always been short of both. The best times were the 1940s, during and immediately after the Second World War. A powerful miners' union, the United Mine Workers (U.M.W.) of America, won considerable gains for all its members, including those of Appalachia.

The miners' leader was an eloquent Welshman named John L. Lewis. Under his leadership the coal miners became one of the best paid groups of workers in the United States, with a guaranteed minimum wage of 24 dollars a day. On top of this Lewis got the mine owners to give 40 cents for every tonne of coal produced to set up a welfare and retirement fund for the miners. Under this scheme U.M.W. members got free medical and hospital care and the best retirement pensions in American industry.

But the good times did not last. In the 1950s competition from alternative fuels like oil and natural gas hit the coal-mining industry. Many less profitable mines were closed down. The owners of the ones that remained cut production costs by bringing in more machines. In eastern Kentucky the number of mining jobs had fallen by almost half by the end of the 1950s. In neighbouring West Virginia things were even worse, with the number of jobs falling from 134,000 to 59,000 in the same period.

Changes like these took place in other coal-mining areas,

both in the United States and in other countries. The thing that made them so serious for the people of Appalachia was that there in the hills there was no other job for the out-of-work miner to turn to. He had only two real choices; to pack up and leave the area, or to go back to his shack in the mountains and live on 'welfare'. Welfare was the handouts of money and food which the government gave to people who were not earning enough to cover essentials like food and rent.

Between 1950 and 1960 nearly 2 million of the people of Appalachia chose the first alternative. Many went north, to cities like Chicago. A nineteen-year-old from Kentucky spoke to a reporter there:

'Chicago, hits a place you can labor and work and make a livin' at. We have better things in life than we did down home. I have everything I can wish for. I still have my mother. I have my stepfather. I have twelve good brothers and two nice sisters. And work every day an' make fine money. I eat good. I can't see anything else a man can ask for. As long as I'm workin' I figure everything'll go O.K.'

For those who stayed behind in Appalachia unemployment became a way of life. Men competed desperately for what work there was, often in non-union mines paying starvation wages of 3 dollars a day. Some even deserted their families so that their wives would be able to get more money in relief payments from the government.

In 1960 John Kennedy visited West Virginia during his campaign for the Presidency. He promised that if he were elected he would do something to try and improve things in Appalachia. He kept his promise from the grave. In 1965, almost two years after his death, Congress passed the Appalachian Regional Development Act.

The Appalachian Regional Development Act gave 1,100 million dollars of government money to be spent on projects agreed upon by the Federal authorities and the state governments of the area. Some of the money went to train ex-miners to do other jobs, some to set up health centres. But the largest share — 840 million dollars — was allocated to build new roads. The idea was to open up Appalachia to the outside world and give it a better chance of attracting new industries and new jobs.

By the mid-1970s it was still not clear if this idea was going to work. One problem was the old one of the lack of established towns. It seemed that factory owners were not keen to go searching out unskilled workers among the hillside cabins of Appalachia when they could set up their factories instead in existing communities already provided with schools, hospitals and shops.

When a reporter from Britain visited Appalachia during the Presidential Election Campaign in the summer of 1976, he found little improvement since a previous visit in 1968.

'Eight years ago, Jessie Taylor in West Virginia...said... that Beverly, her daughter, was ill and should be in hospital but that she and her husband, who had been laid off from the mines, could not afford the hospital bills.

Last week I knocked on Jessie's door again. She is exactly the same, her skin as white as ice from a diet of cheap corn-bread. Her house still has neither bath nor lavatory, just a hole in the ground outside.

"We eventually got Beverly into hospital," said Jessie, "but the bill ran up to 3,000 dollars, so we had to pull her out of there. We're still payin' them off. ..."

In Mercer County, where Jessie lives, there is still no market, no cinema, no regular public transport.

Almost all the children have asthma or lung diseases caused by the unchecked pollution and the local mine company has closed down the company store, so that now people must travel twenty miles to buy meat that other people's pets eat.'

Little wonder that Appalachia was looked upon as a shame, as well as a problem, to the United States.

California

If Appalachia spells poverty to the people of the United States, California spells plenty. And as Appalachia is a place to get away from, California is a place to get to. This is what millions of Americans thought in the years after 1945.

This long narrow state, lying between the western mountains and the shores of the Pacific Ocean (see map on page vi), has been a magnet drawing other Americans westwards ever since the early years of the twentieth century. But in the 1940s the steady flow of people into California turned into a flood. Between 1940 and 1950 the population grew from 6.9 million to 10.6 million. It was not merely a pleasant climate and spectacular scenery that attracted the newcomers. The big appeal of California was well-paid work.

In the early 1940s California became America's front line in the Pacific war against Japan. It had long been a noted farming and fruit-growing state; now it became important for industry too. Factories and houses soon stood where orange and lemon groves had once flourished. One and a half million people moved into the state to man the assembly lines of the fast growing war industries. They in their turn became the customers who attracted other industries and other workers to California. In the later years of the 1940s one out of every eight of all the new businesses set up in the United States was started in the single Californian city of Los Angeles. They made everything — from sliding doors to underwear,

Californian sunshine and prosperity. A street in Los Angeles

from swimsuits to mechanical saws, from scientific instruments to household china.

California continued to grow in the 1950s. Another 3 million people moved in from other parts of the country. It was, claimed the Governor of the state in the early 1960s, 'the greatest mass migration in the history of mankind'. By 1970 California had more people than any other state in the country. The newcomers still came partly for California's sunshine and scenic beauty, for its surf-fringed beaches and its tree-clad mountains. But above all they came because California continued to be a land of opportunity, with plenty of well-paid jobs and the highest living standards in the world.

In 1970 more than nine out of every ten Californians lived in built-up urban areas. Many were clustered around the state's two biggest cities, Los Angeles in the south and San Francisco in the north. These two 'metropolitan areas' were the state's main centres of employment.

Before the Second World War industry in California was dominated by food processing. Jobs such as fruit and vegetable canning gave employment to almost three times as many workers as any other group of industries. But the war changed all this. Most important of all California became the centre of a giant aircraft industry. After the war this expanded into an even bigger group of industries — the huge aero-space complex which grew up as the United States began to explore space in the 1950s and 1960s.

By the early 1970s over a third of all the industrial jobs in the southern part of California, almost half a million of them, were in the aero-space industry. It was estimated that between 10,000 and 12,000 separate firms in the area were connected with aero-space in one way or another. But not even this was the full story. Just as the aircraft industry had given rise to the aero-space industries, so these in their turn bred a new generation of industries in fields like electronics. These put to everyday use the discoveries originally made in the fields of rocketry, missiles and space travel.

California's heavy dependence on the aero-space industries had its dangers. It meant that if the government decided to cut spending on military aircraft or space research, jobs were bound to disappear. In the early 1970s this is exactly what happened. The expeditions to the moon had been completed. The war in Vietnam was dragging to an end. For the first time in over thirty years there was a fall in the number of aero-space jobs. The seemingly endless growth of California's population stopped dead in its tracks. In 1973, for the first time this century, about as many people moved out of California as moved in.

California had other problems by the 1970s. There were racial difficulties, especially in the Los Angeles area. A million Mexicans and three-quarters of a million blacks lived there, most of them in their own districts of the city. Because their standards of education were lower than were required in many of the available jobs, large numbers were out of work.

In 1965 the main black area of Los Angeles, a district called Watts, exploded in an outburst of rage and violence. Thirty-four people were killed, over a thousand injured and an area of 2½ square kilometres was looted and burned out. A government enquiry afterwards fixed a lot of the blame for the riot on lack of work. The unemployment rate for young people in Watts was as high as 25 to 30 per cent. Even for adults the rate was 12 to 15 per cent, half as high again as that for the city's inhabitants as a whole. Although steps were taken to try to improve the situation — new black-run factories moved into Watts, for example — this racially-biased unemployment continued to be a problem.

Another problem worrying Californians was that of the ever-increasing pollution of their natural environment. The state's cities and towns had spread without plan or control across the countryside in an ugly jumble of wooden houses and prefabricated factories. Thousands of hectares of its orchards and farmlands had been swallowed up by multi-laned automobile freeways. Its water had been poisoned by industrial waste, its air by car exhaust fumes. A haze of metallic green chemical smog often hung over Los Angeles, stinging the eyes and shutting out the sun. 'The great things that brought people to California were climate and jobs', commented one resident in the 1970s, 'and now they've both gone to hell.'

But most Californians were convinced that these problems

of the 1970s were just a passing phase. For them California was still 'the golden state', a land of unlimited promise.

New York

'New York, New York, it's a wonderful town!' So began a popular song of the 1940s. At the time few Americans would have argued with the statement. Thirty years later things had changed. A reporter told of a tourist visiting New York from the mid-western state of Kansas in 1972. The tourist took a good look at the most famous city in the United States and declared in disgust: 'this is not America. This is a jungle.'

New York City is situated on the east coast of the United States at the mouth of the Hudson River (see map on page vi). The city sprawls for many kilometres, but its heart is the island of Manhattan. Manhattan is just over 3 kilometres long and 3 kilometres wide and its business is business. In one skyscraper block alone, newly opened in 1974, there was space for 50,000 workers. Every day 1½ million people stream to work there, over the bridges and through the tunnels which connect the island to the land around.

A third of all the office space in the United States was

'New York, New York, it is a wonderful town'. But by the 1970s it was overcrowded, dirty, dangerous — and bankrupt

crowded onto Manhattan in the 1970s. Thirty-one of the country's biggest industrial firms had their headquarters there. So did ten of the fifty biggest banks, six of the biggest insurance companies, eight of the biggest transport firms and all three of the nation's main television networks. They had all come here because New York is the financial heart of the United States. New York is where the decisions are made, New York is where the power is.

And yet, in the 1970s, many people feared that New York was dying. It seemed that its problems had grown too big for anyone to handle.

One of these problems was jobs. After rising steadily in the 1950s and 1960s, the number of jobs in the city started to fall dramatically in the 1970s. More and more firms moved out, from small dress-making businesses to giant corporations like Shell and Pepsico. One reason for this was cost. Space on Manhattan was the most expensive on earth. In the early 1970s, even to garage a car there could cost £150 a month.

But money was not the main reason why people were leaving New York. Far more important was the increasing unpleasantness of everyday life there. The canyon-like streets between the skyscrapers were polluted by exhaust fumes and noise. It became dangerous to walk the streets at night for fear of being attacked and robbed. Overcrowding turned every day into a ceaseless struggle to find space to sit, to eat, to move, even to stand. 'The truly terrible costs of New York are endless human discomfort, inconvenience, harassment and fear', wrote one observer. 'These things have become part of the background, like the noise and the filth but much deadlier. ... If people are driven and their senses dulled, if they are de-humanised, the city is on the way to destroying itself.'

A black artist put a similar point of view more briefly. 'Its a heavy scene here. I've had it. I'm so tired of being scared.' A single statistic illustrates his point. In the early 1970s New York had as many murders every ten days as the whole of England suffered in a year.

And so, the people who could afford to moved out of the city — 1½ million of them, mostly middle-class whites, between 1950 and 1970. They left behind them the people who couldn't afford to move — poor, unskilled and mostly black families. Other unskilled black and brown families moved in to join them. Many came from Puerto Rico, a Spanish-speaking island in the Caribbean Sea governed by the United States. Most hoped to find jobs, others were attracted by the city's high level of welfare payments. In the early 1970s almost 1¼ million people in New York were living on welfare — this was one-seventh of the city's population.

By the 1970s New York, like many more big American cities, was divided on racial and social lines into distinct areas. Poor blacks lived in the centre and prosperous whites on the outskirts. In between lived the less well-off working-class whites. Because the people living in the centre of the city were so poor, they paid far less in taxes to the city government than the people who used to live there. The result was that the city authorities did not have enough money coming in to pay for vital public services. Rubbish piled up in alleyways, waiting to be picked up, streets were dirty and potholed, the subway or underground railway system was overcrowded and continually breaking down. On top of all this there was an acute shortage of decent houses and of school and hospital places.

By the middle of the 1970s the city of New York was bank-rupt, it simply could not pay its way. To many people there seemed to be only one solution to the problem — money from the Federal Government.

John Lindsay, the Mayor of New York from 1966 to 1974, pointed out that cities like New York provided valuable ser-vices for the whole nation and not just for the people who lived there. He claimed, therefore, that New York and other cities with similar problems had every right to claim money from the national purse to help them to solve their difficul-ties. But national leaders, such as President Reagan, dis-agreed with him and New York's financial problems continued to be a headache for the mayors who followed Lindsay.

Nevertheless, New York continued to be 'a wonderful town' to many of its citizens. Yes, they admitted, their city was dirty, it was overcrowded, it was dangerous. But they still took a curious pride in it.

12 Farming and the Farmers

Family Farming and Agribusiness

Farming is the biggest industry in the United States. Not oil, or steel, or car producing but farming. Half the country's land area is used to raise crops or animals. In the 1970s American farms were producing half the world's maize, a third of its oats, a fifth of its chickens, a sixth of its wheat and a tenth of its pigs.

Jim Jamisson is in many ways a typical American farmer. In the early 1970s he supported his wife and family by running a 'family farm' — that is, one upon which he did most of the work himself. The Jamisson farm is in the maize-growing state of Iowa, on the deep rich soil which covers a vast area of the middle part of the United States. Because maize, or corn as Americans call it, is the main crop all over this area, it is often referred to as the Corn Belt.

The size of Jim Jamisson's farm was about average for the United States — 153 hectares. The money he earned from it was less than he might have got from working in a factory, but it was enough to give him and his family a comfortable life. To keep down his costs he had to be a jack of all trades. He put right his machinery when it went wrong and he did the repairs on his house and farm buildings. He also had to know about the latest farming ideas and methods, so that he could make use of any new discoveries that might be useful to him. His grandfather had tilled the land using a mule to pull his plough. Jim turned over the same soil with a tractor. His grandfather sowed the same kind of corn seed for years. Jim used high-yielding hybrid varieties developed in scientific laboratories by research workers. Jim also relied upon other aids which his grandfather had never dreamed of — chemical fertilizers, pesticides, weedkillers and a host of specialized machines.

106

Cedar Falls, Iowa, 1976. A family farm on the Corn Belt

The main effect of all these changes was greatly to increase the amount that Jim Jamisson produced, compared with his grandfather. Grandfather had raised enough food to feed eight people. On the same land, Jim Jamisson raised enough for forty-five.

In the 1970s a large part of the agricultural produce of the United States was being turned out on family farms like Jim Jamisson's. But there were fewer such farms then than there had been. In the thirty years after 1945 a total of 3 million small independent farmers gave up their land. By 1975 the farming population of the United States had dwindled to about 9.5 million people, compared with more than 30 million in 1935. As these people moved out, their land was usually taken over by neighbouring farmers who added it to their own. The result was that the number of farms got smaller but their average size got bigger, increasing from about 62 hectares in 1935 to 150 hectares in 1975.

At the other end of the scale from family farms like Jim Jamisson's were the growing number that were owned or controlled by big business corporations. A list of leading

American farmers of the 1970s would have included, for example, such unlikely names as the Boeing Aircraft Corporation and the Greyhound Bus Line. For firms like these their farming activities were a sideline, a way of investing some of the profits made in their main line of business. This did not mean that they played at farming and failed to take it seriously. Far from it. The corporations set out to bring to farming the methods and business efficiency of large-scale industry. For this reason their kind of farming was soon being referred to as 'agribusiness'.

In the mid-1970s only one American farm in every hundred was of the agribusiness kind. But they controlled 8 per cent of the total farm area and were doing almost 15 per cent of the total amount of farm business. What is more, these percentages were growing.

This growth of agribusiness worried some Americans. For the whole of the 200 years that the United States had existed, small family farmers had been looked upon by many as the nation's backbone — hard-working, independent and self-reliant, people who acted as a valuable stabilizing influence on society. To protect them from being swallowed up by agribusiness, by the mid-1970s a number of states had passed laws forbidding big business corporations to take up farming and several others were thinking of doing the same.

The Farmer and the Government

One of the modern American farmer's biggest problems is not how to grow more plentiful crops, but how to get a good price for those crops when he has grown them.

In the twentieth century the prosperity of the American farmer has gone up and down like a yo-yo. His troubles really started in the 1920s, after the First World War. While other Americans prospered the farmers had a hard time. During the world-wide trade depression of the 1930s things got even worse. By 1933 the selling prices of most crops were so low that many farmers were leaving them to rot in the fields because they could not afford to harvest them.

After 1933 President Franklin Roosevelt's New Deal policies started to make things better for the farmers. But it was the Second World War that really put them on their feet. Wartime food shortages meant that they could sell every-thing they could produce at a good price. These good times continued after the fighting stopped. To keep up the prices of their crops when the wartime shortages ended, the farmers got their representatives in Congress to persuade the govern-ment to give money to ensure that they got a minimum price for their produce. These payments, or subsidies, took a num-ber of forms. Sometimes the government paid the farmers not to grow certain crops, as Roosevelt had done. More impor-tant for the future though, the government sometimes bought the farmers' products itself and put them into store.

In the 1950s government purchases of surplus crops started to pile up all over the United States. By June 1956 it was estimated that more than 8 billion dollars worth of crops were in store. It seemed that no matter how much the Amer-ican exporter sold or the American government gave away, the surpluses went on growing.

What to do about the massive crop surpluses continued to be a problem for American governments all through the 1960s. But in the 1970s the surpluses at last began to fall. A major reason for this was a series of crop failures in other parts of the world. These led to huge purchases of American grain by other countries such as the Soviet Union. For the first time that anyone could remember, American farmers were unable to produce as much wheat and maize as custom-ers all over the world wanted to buy.

How long this world-wide demand for American foodstuffs would last was a question no one could answer. As they gathered in their most profitable harvests ever American far-mers wondered what the future held for them. Would it be one in which the twentieth-century world's chronic food shortage would ensure that they found customers for all they could grow? Or would it be one in which only further hand-outs from the government would save them from being ruined by their own efficiency and productivity?

The Other Farmers

Not all American farmers and farm workers were well off in

Salinas, California, 1976. Chicano field workers harvesting lettuce

the years after 1945. Many worked farms that were too small to give them a decent living. Others couldn't afford the machines to make their work easier and more profitable. Worst off of all were the Chicanos. The Chicanos were workers from Mexico who harvested the crops of the orchards and vegetable fields of California's rich Central Valley. Many were illegal immigrants, who had slipped unnoticed across the border from Mexico in search of work.

For years the Chicanos were afraid to stand up for their rights for fear of being arrested and sent back to Mexico. The result was that they worked in some of the worst conditions and for the lowest wages in the United States. In the 1960s Cesar Chavez set out to change this. Chavez was of Mexican origin himself and in 1962 he set up the United Farm Workers' Union (U.F.W) to help the Chicanos. He persuaded them to go on strike to force employers to give them better

wages and conditions. He added to the pressure on the growers by persuading people all over the United States to refuse
to buy Californian grapes and other crops.

The strikes and the boycotts went on for years, but in 1970
the growers gave in and signed agreements with the U.F.W.
These contracts gave the Chicano field workers the second
highest agricultural wage rates in the world. They also gave
them other benefits, such as free medical care and strict safety regulations to protect them against the dangerous pesticides sprayed on the crops. Most important of all perhaps,
La Causa — 'the Cause', as Chavez called his campaign —
gave the Chicanos a degree of dignity and self respect.

But the struggle was far from finished. To his followers
Chavez was a saint, but to the growers he was a half crazy
fanatic whose demands were threatening to ruin their business. In 1973 many of the growers made a deal with the
Teamsters' Union — the biggest and most corrupt in the
country. The Teamsters accepted lower wages for the workers than the growers had agreed with Chavez and the
U.F.W.'s health regulations were quietly dropped. In return,
the growers agreed to pay 1½ million dollars a year directly
into the Teamsters' Union's central funds.

Gangs of Teamster strong-arm men moved into the fruit
and vegetable fields to enforce the new deal with threats and
violence. 'When the Teamsters came I had no choice', one
Chicano worker told a reporter. 'It was either support them
or lose my job. I have to live.'

In the middle 1970s the U.F.W. was fighting for its life.
But by then a threat to the whole world of the Chicano field
worker had appeared in the fields of California. Mechanized
harvesters moved across fields where previously only the
bent backs of the Chicanos had been seen. It seemed that the
last American refuge of the unskilled farm worker was about
to disappear.

13 Blacks and Whites

The Struggle for Civil Rights

'How should we punish Hitler?' a reporter asked a young American black girl towards the end of the Second World War. 'Paint him black and bring him over here', was her bitter reply. It sprang from a lifetime of being treated as a second-class human being. Of being told no, you can't attend this school, have this job, eat in this restaurant, sit on this park bench. And the reason? Because your skin was black.

The official term for all this was segregation — that is, singling out the blacks from the rest of the community and denying them many of the rights enjoyed by other people.

In 1940 10 million of the country's total black population of 13 million lived in the southern United States, most of them in great poverty. By 1970, the picture had changed. The country's total black population was now 24 million or so and 12 million lived outside the south, most of them in big northern industrial cities. A mass migration had taken place. At a steady annual rate of about 150,000 people, more than 4½ million blacks had caught buses and trains out of the south to the north and to California.

The big attraction for the migrants was well-paid jobs in the booming factories of cities like Chicago, Pittsburgh and Detroit. But there was another. Taking the road north or west promised an escape not just from poverty, but from the miseries and humiliations of segregation which were a daily part of every southern black's life. As one black migrant wrote, 'I don't care where so long as I go where a man is a man.'

During the Second World War segregation started to break down, at least outside the south. Black workers earned more money than ever before working alongside whites in the busy wartime factories. Black servicemen not only fought and died, but ate and slept alongside their white fellow countrymen. 'One thing is certain', wrote an observer in 1946. 'The days of treating negroes like sheep are done with. They cannot be maintained in a submerged position because they are now strong enough to contest this position.'

An important legal turning point came in the middle 1950s. In the United States a group of judges called the Supreme Court has the power to say whether a law is legal or not. In 1954 the Supreme Court declared that segregated schools were illegal and ordered that black children should be allowed to enrol as pupils at any school. When black children tried to do this in a southern town called Little Rock, however, an angry mob gathered to prevent them. President Eisenhower sent troops to enforce the Supreme Court decision and the children were admitted. So began a long struggle for equal educational rights, which was still going on more than twenty-five years later.

Little Rock 1957. White students look on as troops escort young blacks into the previously all white High School

The next landmark in the black struggle came on 1 December 1955 when Mrs. Rosa Parks got on a bus in the strictly segregated southern city of Montgomery, Alabama. She took a seat towards the back of the bus, as blacks like her were supposed to do. But then white workers and shoppers filled up the front section of the bus and the driver ordered her to give up her seat. Suddenly Mrs. Parks decided that she had been pushed around enough. She refused, and made up her mind 'never to move again'.

Mrs. Parks was arrested, but the black community of Montgomery rallied to her support. Led by a young Baptist clergyman named Martin Luther King they began a boycott of the city's bus services. The boycott went on for a year until at last the money the city authorities were losing in fares forced them to give in. Montgomery's public transport system was desegregated.

The success of the Montgomery bus boycott encouraged blacks everywhere to act together against the injustices of segregation. They boycotted stores where black workers were refused jobs, organized rent strikes to bring action to improve their often terrible housing conditions, held 'sit-ins' in segregated restaurants. Under the calm but determined leadership of Martin Luther King they achieved many successes. The climax to their campaigning came in August 1963, when 200,000 people, black and white, took part in a mass march to Washington to demand full racial equality.

By this time John Kennedy was President. He sympathized strongly with the blacks and worked out a plan to ensure that all Americans, whatever their race, would receive equal treatment. Kennedy sent his scheme to Congress to be made into a law. He was murdered before this could happen, but his successor, Lyndon Johnson, made getting the law passed one of his first objectives. In 1964 the Civil Rights Act became the law of the land.

From Civil Rights to Black Power

Many Americans hoped that the passing of the Civil Rights Act in 1964 would mark the beginning of a new age of racial harmony and friendship in the United States.

They were disappointed. The racial difficulties of the United States were too deep rooted to be solved by simple alterations in the law, or by peaceful demonstrations and marches. Changes were needed in human attitudes and in underlying economic conditions.

In the 1960s most American blacks were still worse housed, worse educated and worse paid than the rest of the community. Some gave up hope of ever getting a better deal. They decided that blacks would only get decent treatment if certain areas of the country were set on one side for their use alone. This despairing and impractical policy was supported by a group called the Black Muslims. The Muslims rejected with contempt the ideas of moderate leaders like Martin Luther King that blacks and whites should learn to live together side by side in equality and friendship. 'There are many of my poor, black ignorant brothers preaching the ignorant and lying stuff that you should love your enemy', proclaimed their leader. 'What fool can love his enemy?'

The Black Muslims were only a minority. But other black Americans were becoming increasingly impatient at their lack of progress towards real equality and especially towards economic equality. In the hot summers of the mid-1960s this impatience boiled over into violence. In city after city — Los

Los Angeles, 1965. A blood-soaked looting suspect shot by police in the Watts riots

Angeles, Chicago, New York, Detroit — rioters ran wild through the black quarters, looting and burning. (You can read more about the Los Angeles riot in the California section of Chapter 11.) When police and troops moved in to restore order they were fired on by roof-top snipers.

When a black leader was asked about the wave of violence he commented simply, 'If a man's standing on your toe and you've petitioned, begged, pleaded, done everything possible and he won't move — you've got to push him off.' Other blacks agreed with him, especially after 4 April 1968. On that day the peace-loving Martin Luther King was murdered, shot dead on the balcony of a motel in Memphis, Tennessee, by a white sniper. Many blacks now turned to the violent Black Power movement, which taught that the only way blacks would get justice was by fighting for it.

Black People and Black Voices

'Say it loud, I'm black and proud!' The singer spread his arms and screamed the words into the microphone. His audience went wild, surging to the stage to shake his hand or just get close to him. He was James Brown (otherwise known as Mr. Dynamite or Soul Brother Number One), one of the most popular black American singers of the 1960s.

James Brown's song was one of his biggest hits. Yet only a few years earlier it would have been an insult to call a dark skinned American a black. Black was then a dirty word; polite people spoke of négroes or coloured people. In the 1960s, however, Americans with African blood in their veins discovered a new pride in their ancestry. As James Brown advised, they said it loud, they were black and proud. Before long the most frequently seen and heard slogan in America was the three words: 'Black is beautiful'.

This new black pride and self-respect showed itself in many ways. It became fashionable to take African names, to wear long African robes and short African jackets called dasheks. Bushy African hairstyles became the rage of black America and even caught on with white youngsters.

But black pride and racial awareness showed itself in more than dress and appearance. Schools were established which

116

'Black and proud.' Arthur Mitchell rehearses the Dance Theatre of Harlem

taught the pupils the history, the languages and the customs of their African ancestors. One of the most striking ventures was a ballet school set up by a young black dancer named Arthur Mitchell. In Mitchell's school youngsters from the streets of New York's Harlem learned to create new and exciting dances which combined the techniques of classical ballet with the beat of African drums. Within a few years they had become internationally famous as the Dance Theatre of Harlem, playing to packed theatres all over the world.

There were other black success stories. There was the comedian, Dick Gregory, making black and white audiences laugh with stories of his experiences in the civil rights movement. 'I sat at a counter at a restaurant in Alabama for six months. When they finally integrated and I saw the menu, they didn't have what I wanted.' There was the world's heavyweight boxing champion, Muhammad Ali, an outspoken follower of the Black Muslims. There was James Brown, with his 500 suits, his Rolls Royce and his private jet.

Another successful Brown was the film actor, Jim Brown. Good-looking, and intelligent, Jim Brown believed that green power, not black power, was the way forward for his people. Green is the colour of dollar bills and what Brown meant

117

was that racial equality would only grow out of economic equality. The root of the blacks' problem was not that they were black, but that they were poor; that they hadn't got 'enough of the green'. Another man made a similar point in these words: 'I'm past Black is Beautiful. I want what every other American wants — a body full of food and a pocket full of money.'

But not all blacks saw the problem in such basic, perhaps over simple terms. Some had different, more idealistic aims. Eldridge Cleaver, a leader of a revolutionary group called the Black Panthers, rejected the materialism of the capitalist society of the United States completely. To him to be 'black and proud' was just a beginning:

'Regaining your black identity does not necessarily set you free. We have got to rid ourselves of this dreadful and consuming hunger for things, this mindless substitution of the rat race for human life. Only then will people become capable of relating to other people on the basis of individual merit... The values I stand for are really quite traditional and simple — like respecting your fellow man. These goals are as old as time itself. Let people be. Let people fulfil their capacities.'

Arthur Mitchell was a dancer not a revolutionary. His ways of trying to improve the position of his fellow blacks were very different from Eldridge Cleaver's. Yet his underlying view of people, of their hopes and needs, was not so very different from that of Cleaver, or of Martin Luther King, or even of Jim Brown. 'I used to be full of anger', he told a reporter when the Dance Theatre of Harlem visited London in 1976, 'but not any more. Screams and yells don't get you anywhere. I discovered that black or white, green or purple, all kids are the same. People are the same. I don't think of myself as a black man, first and foremost. I'm just a man who happens to be black.'

The best hope for racial justice and peace in the United States was that perhaps, in time, enough other people, black and white, would come to think the same.

Conclusion

In 1976 the United States celebrated its two-hundredth anniversary as an independent nation. As it entered its third century of existence there were unmistakable signs that after the turmoil of unrest that the country had gone through in the later 1960s, the American people were ready for a breather. Most were not interested in crusading against communism, or in campaigning for social reforms, in struggling to cross 'new frontiers', or to create 'great societies'. What they wanted was a period of quiet and stability in which they could get on with the job of providing themselves and their families with secure and comfortable lives.

These average Americans knew better than anyone that their country had problems. They, after all, had to live with them — with the racial unrest, the crime on the streets, the twin threats of unemployment and inflation. But although they worried and complained about such things, in their hearts they believed that the American way of life was basically sound. Whatever the difficulties, they felt, the United States would eventually overcome them. Given the choice, few would have lived anywhere else.

Index